SPIRIT

HUAWEI STORIES

TIAN TAO
YIN ZHIFENG

Published by
LID Publishing Limited
The Record Hall, Studio 304,
16-16a Baldwins Gardens,
London EC1N 7RJ, UK

info@lidpublishing.com
www.lidpublishing.com

A member of:

businesspublishersroundtable.com

Printed by CPI Group (UK) Ltd, Croydon CR0 4YY
ISBN: 978-1-911671-03-9
ISBN: 978-1-911671-37-4 (ebook)

Cover and page design: Caroline Li

SPIRIT

HUAWEI STORIES

TIAN TAO
YIN ZHIFENG

MADRID | MEXICO CITY | LONDON
NEW YORK | BUENOS AIRES
BOGOTA | SHANGHAI | NEW DELHI

Contents

Foreword

Attracting Huge Numbers of Geniuses

Excerpts from Comments by Huawei Founder and CEO Ren Zhengfei at the 20-Minute Sharing Session of the Executive Management Team Meeting[1]

Every department in the company must create a favourable environment that removes all unnecessary constraints, realizes the full potential of all employees, and encourages them to remain dedicated and forge ahead. Moving into the future, Huawei will move the world forward and set new standards. As long as we are the best in the world, our standards will be followed by others.

This year, we will hire 20–30 top minds from around the world, and we plan to bring another 200–300 to Huawei next year. We expect these individuals to galvanize and inspire passion across our organization.

What is a genius? A genius is someone who makes breakthroughs in a specific domain. We must remember that a jack-of-all-trades is a master of none. After solid foundations are laid in certain domains, geniuses can seize the opportunities and identify the domains in which they can make breakthroughs. However, we find that the domains they choose are often not the areas they prepared themselves for. Those who merely attend classes and complete assignments can never be considered geniuses.

We must attract a huge number of geniuses. Chu Kochen, the former president of China's Zhejiang University, created the university's motto: 'Seeking the Truth and Pioneering New Trails.' This has enabled a considerable number of geniuses to emerge from the school. Huawei must do the same to attract such geniuses who, in turn, will help bring even more talent to Huawei.

For example, international computer competitions around the world produce only 40 gold medal winners each year, and we should recruit all of them. However, the 400 contestants who make it to the finals of the competitions every year are also very talented. Therefore, I think we can hire all of them, even if they have not won top prizes.

The Gauss Squirrel Club is a fantastic platform, which is designed to review database development and improve the understanding of databases. Other small business-centred clubs can also be established at Huawei to give employees opportunities to share their passions and hobbies.

I didn't allow such clubs at the company in the past, regarding them only as places for unofficial activities. However, I now think the Human Resource Management Department should conduct

I believe our company
will be completely
different in three to
five years, and that we
will have everything
we need to succeed.
Who should we rely on
to make this a reality?
Our geniuses.

some research into how to make these clubs official. Harvard University has thousands of these clubs, which serve as platforms for academic discussions and exchanges. Through such clubs, we can absorb the energy of the universe over a cup of coffee, and bring huge numbers of geniuses together.

The Greek philosopher Socrates spoke to many people in many places. His work influenced the establishment of the Roman Forum and he was essential to the development of numerous Western philosophies. At Huawei, we can encourage employees to drink coffee and exchange ideas with people both inside and outside of the company.

Employees can post publicly available papers they read on our internal messaging board, Xinsheng Community, and on the bulletin board of Huawei University so that other employees can also study these papers. Some of the papers can even be published on external websites to share with other companies.

I also call on our geniuses to invite their outstanding classmates and friends to join Huawei, where they can achieve something great together. We should not be concerned about them forming cliques, as they will work closely together and forge ahead no matter what challenges stand in their way. For anyone who successfully brings a genius to Huawei, I will personally invite them out for a coffee.

I believe our company will be completely different in three to five years, and that we will have everything we need to succeed. Who should we rely on to make this a reality? Our geniuses.

With geniuses joining Huawei in large numbers, there will be no challenges we cannot overcome. We invest everything in the future and have the courage to expand, and this attracts many geniuses to join us. If Huawei can serve as a 'string' that ties together the 'pearls' – geniuses – around the world to make a 'necklace,' we will become a world leader.

1   After discussions at a meeting of the Executive Management Team (EMT) –
    Huawei's most senior leadership team – on March 29, 2018, Huawei added a
    special item to the agenda of the monthly EMT meetings: a 20-Minute Sharing
    Session. This session encourages employees to share their work achievements and
    experience; the goal is to enhance communication between management and
    employees, and drive outstanding talent to stand out. Two employees participate
    at every session, each giving a 10-minute presentation. Any Huawei employees can
    apply to give a presentation at these sessions and share what they have achieved
    at work. They must only share things they have actually experienced themselves.
    Employees can directly submit applications to a designated email account without
    going through level-by-level approvals. On 29 July 2019, Ye Huihui and Ren Yang
    spoke at a session. Ye Huihui holds a bachelor's degree from the Nanchang Institute
    of Technology, and joined Huawei in October 2013. He is assigned to the East
    African island nation of Comoros, and has gone from being an account manager
    to the head of Huawei's Comoros Office. Ren Yang holds a PhD from Zhejiang
    University, and joined Huawei in September 2014. He has grown from an R&D
    engineer into a senior technical expert.

A Man,
A Cook
and A Dog

By Ye Huihui

"I'm Ye Huihui from the Comoros Office …"

"Wait. Where is Comoros? I've never been there."

When I was delivering a presentation during the 20-minute Sharing Session at the meeting of the Executive Management Team – Huawei's most senior leadership team – in July 2019, founder and CEO Ren Zhengfei interrupted me just as I began introducing myself.

Where is Comoros? I had asked this very same question six years ago. It didn't occur to me that this island country in the Indian Ocean – which I used to know nothing about and never thought I would have any connection to – would become the most indispensable part of my life.

In fact, when I first arrived in Comoros, nothing was as I had imagined. I actually felt regret the moment I arrived.

I was disconnected from the rest of the world

At the end of 2013, I came to Comoros for the first time. I was 24 years old back then and had been at Huawei for less than one month.

I came with a colleague from the project delivery department. A local driver picked us up from the airport in a pickup truck and drove us to our dormitory. Outside the window, I saw worn-down buildings and streets on both sides of the road. They looked even worse than those in the African country where I used to work. I started feeling a little worried.

Before joining Huawei, I had worked in Côte d'Ivoire for two years. One of my friends who worked at Huawei had tried very hard to persuade me to join the company. He said I would achieve something great at Huawei. He told me later on that he would get a ¥6,000 bonus for successfully getting me to join the company. No wonder he had tried so hard to persuade me!

After joining Huawei, I was assigned to the Madagascar Office. After working there for about 20 days, my manager told me that the submarine cable project we had been working on in Comoros for years had been resumed recently. He asked me to provide onsite support there as an account manager.

"Where is Comoros?" This was the first time that I had ever heard of it. My manager gave me some information, and I learned that this island nation was located between the African continent and Madagascar and had a small population of just 800,000. The local economy was underdeveloped and the infrastructure was poor. This submarine cable project meant a lot to Comoros, and was expected to connect the country with the rest of the world.

I said yes to my manager without any hesitation. I had just joined Huawei, and lacked product knowledge and experience, but my manager trusted me and I had to take this opportunity to prove myself. Although I didn't know much about Comoros, I had already worked in Africa, where I learned French by myself and even once contracted malaria. Our working conditions in the Madagascar Office were much better compared with my previous experiences, so I got on the plane and couldn't wait to explore this unknown country.

Before I set off, one of my colleagues told me that life in Comoros was very difficult. Electricity was only available for one or two hours every day and communications signals were very weak. He also told me that the local people had to connect to the internet through dial-up access, using Asymmetric Digital Subscriber Line (ADSL) technology, and they were basically disconnected from the rest of the world. I didn't think it would really bother me, but when I arrived at the dormitory I found myself in surroundings that were a vast contrast to modern civilization. The conditions of the dormitory were much poorer than those in Madagascar. It had been left unrepaired for years and the facilities were rundown. Water and electricity were scarcely available.

I took out my phone to make an international long-distance call to my parents in China and tell them I was safe. But the call was disconnected as soon as I attempted to call my mum. I didn't want my parents to worry about me, so I made dozens more calls, but none of them got through. I found out later that my mum had also tried calling me hundreds of times, and got really worried about me until she finally reached one of my colleagues and was reassured that I was safe.

It was around 8 pm, and my bedroom was dark due to a lack of electricity. With the help of the dim light on my phone, I managed to locate my bed. I decided to sit down and take a rest, but the bed suddenly fell apart, and the loud noise shocked my colleagues and the local driver. They came over and helped me put the bed back together. Then we went out for dinner with the local Chinese medical team.

After this dinner, I learned more about this country and became more upset. I had been overly optimistic. Comoros is one of the world's least developed countries, with scarce living supplies, extremely outdated infrastructure, and rampant malaria and dengue fever. In addition to the lack of water and electricity, there was a serious shortage of fruits and vegetables. The country is mostly rocky volcanic land, which isn't good for agriculture.

Why on earth had I decided to come to this country? The sharp contrast between my high expectations and the bleak reality kept me awake during my first night in Comoros. I tossed and turned, and felt remorse. But I still clearly remembered how I had gladly promised my manager I would come here. I said to myself, "Now that I'm here, I should start working."

Eighteen ways to eat tuna

A lack of water and electricity was the first obstacle that stood in my way as I tried to settle down in Comoros.

These difficulties were not a big issue during daytime, when I could go to the customer's equipment room to power my devices and connect to the internet. But when night came, I had to go back to my dormitory, where there was only one hour of electricity available every night. This hour was very precious to me, and I had to finish many tasks within this short period of time, including boiling water, cooking and bathing.

My bathing procedures in Comoros were very crude: I would fill a bucket of water from the cistern, take the bucket to the bathroom and use a water scoop to pour water on my body. Although I was born in a rural village in China, the bathing facilities at home when I was a child were still much better than those in my dormitory.

Within this one-hour time span, I also had to charge my phone and torch. I would then usually lie in bed and meditate or do some writing by the desk, which was a way to talk to myself. The Indian Ocean breeze, the starry sky and the classical music from my phone helped put my mind at ease.

One night, when the power was out, a local colleague took out a guitar and started playing. I joined in, playing the harmonica. Other local colleagues turned on their phone flashlights, and danced and sang to our tune. This beautiful scene is still fresh in my mind today.

Food shortages were another challenge, and I have another interesting story related to this. On the day I set off to Comoros, I met with a delivery colleague at the Madagascar airport, and gave him a boxed meal made by the cook in our local office as lunch. He kept this box and brought it directly to Comoros. I thought he had done this because he wasn't hungry, but later found that he reserved the meal because he had been to Comoros before and knew there would be little for us to eat there. This food was so delicious and precious to us that my colleague and I made it into two meals on the following day.

Comoros suffers from serious food shortages. In addition to the local speciality – tuna – the country imports frozen beef and chicken, and there are also cassava, bananas and coconuts. Given the scarcity of fresh fruits and vegetables, every time a colleague visited, they would bring some with them. I remember that one day, not long after I arrived in Comoros, a Chinese product manager came on a business trip and brought two cabbages with him. It had been a while since I had eaten green vegetables, and I was thrilled. We ate one cabbage that night and saved the other for another day. We put it in the refrigerator, only to find it had gone rotten a few days later as the refrigerator had been powered off and the temperature was so high. Both the product manager and I were very upset by this.

It was not until the second half of 2014 that our business in Comoros started picking up. So, the company officially set up an office in Comoros and even hired a Chinese cook. I was the only Chinese employee who had been working in the country for a relatively long time, so people joked about me being a privileged individual who had my own cook.

The cook, Wang, was in his 50s and was like an elder brother who treated us like family. He made excellent Sichuan cuisine, and Huawei's canteen earned the reputation of 'the best Chinese restaurant in Comoros.' Take tuna as an example. Wang could prepare 18 different tuna dishes: steamed, red braised, vinegar flavoured, barbecued and many more. He even had a tuna dish that tasted like chicken, and we called it 'tuna chicken.'

What touched me most about Wang was that he would always save food for latecomers. He told us that only when you have a full stomach you will stop being homesick. That's why Wang would always check who was absent at mealtimes and would save something for them. And the saved portion was usually double the norm. Once a delivery guy returned from a customer office after 10 pm. When he was having the hot meal, he started sobbing. Wang asked what had happened. The delivery guy said, with tears in his eyes, "It tastes so good!"

The sea around Comoros

Customers became our close friends

By the time I arrived there in 2013, the Comorian market had been long monopolized by Western vendors. As a Chinese Information and Communications Technology (ICT) company, Huawei did not have much credibility with local customers. They thought Western products were the best and the most advanced. I was a newcomer at the time and didn't have much knowledge about local business or Huawei products. My French was also not that good, and Comoros is a French-speaking country. So in the beginning it was extremely difficult for me to develop business.

The CEO of one customer did not want to meet with me. I once waited from the afternoon until 1 am the next day outside his office. When I finally managed to see the CEO, I talked with him in my broken French mixed with some English words. I was hoping he would give me a chance to sit down and talk. He looked at me, shook his head, and left. Exhausted and hungry, I watched him walking away. I was extremely frustrated and could hardly keep the tears at bay.

The harsh environment and slow progress at work stressed me out, and I was at a total loss, but what happened later changed my mind.

The only means of transportation between the islands in Comoros were propeller-driven airplanes or motorboats. One day, I accompanied a customer to one of the neighbouring islands by plane to inspect sites, but we encountered a thunderstorm while in the air. The propeller stopped at one point, and the plane plummeted. I thought the plane was going to crash, but, fortunately, it landed safely. But this intense weightlessness cast a psychological shadow over me. That's why I chose a motorboat the next time I went to that island with a colleague.

The trip to the island was smooth, and our customer signed the contract, leaving us really uplifted. On our way back, we took a motorboat again. But soon after we set out, dark clouds gathered quickly in the clear and boundless sky above the sea. A storm would come soon.

There were four people on the motorboat: my colleague, a local woman, the helmsman and me. We quickly put on the ragged life jackets, even though they would not really help. We just wanted to comfort ourselves. This was the first time that I had ever experienced a sea storm. It was really scary. The wind and rain were getting more and more intense. I couldn't tell whether it was seawater or rain splashing my face. I couldn't even keep my eyes open.

Our boat was too small to withstand such a heavy storm. It was being swept here and there by the wind and waves. I thought we were going to capsize.

We were terrified, and the local woman was praying for protection. I was desperate and helpless: How could we survive if we fell into the sea? I had been lucky that the plane had not crashed the last time, but could I make it this time?

I really wanted to cry, and my heart was filled with regret. Why had I chosen to come to Comoros? This place was so harsh, and now even my life was at stake!

Despite the fear, I still had a clear head. I was holding this important contract, so I hurriedly put the folder underneath all of the layers I was wearing because that was the only way to try to keep it dry. This contract should now be on file at our company's headquarters in Bantian, Shenzhen, and that's how it got the yellow water stains.

Fortunately, the storm passed as quickly as it came. Our desperation and fright didn't last long. The dark clouds dispersed and the sea calmed. I was stunned by what I saw as I stood on the deck: there were two magnificent rainbows arching across the horizon. It was the first time I had seen such a magnificent scene, and I had an unforgettable realization: life is so precious, and I am so lucky to be the master of my own destiny. I realized at that moment that I must control my own future, and face the difficulties in my life head-on.

So I started changing. I worked harder to learn French, memorizing a lot of words every day. I managed to read through all the books that our French language majors used in college. I even badgered a local colleague into practising spoken French with me. When I was in the customer's equipment room to power my devices and connect to the internet during daytime, I also took the opportunity to 'stumble across' customer employees and talk with them. Maybe I'm secretly gifted at languages; I became able to talk with customers in French at a good level, very quickly! Meanwhile, I worked hard to study business management and product knowledge, and presented what I learned to different levels of customers. I gave presentations to many customers, ranging from engineers all the way up to government ministers and the country's president.

When I communicate with customers, I'm not eager to sell Huawei products and services. Instead, I first try to make friends with them and sincerely show how communications can make a difference in society. I still remember that when I introduced a videoconferencing system, I told the customers that with a good network and this system, we could have face-to-face meetings with people from all around the world, and we no longer had to travel back and forth across different islands for meetings. This deeply impressed the customers, some of whom had even fallen into the sea when travelling by motorboat. In addition, since we had operated there for a long time and had a stable local maintenance team, Huawei could offer on-demand services to our customers, something other vendors couldn't do. After seeing Huawei's sincerity and strengths, the customers started to work with us, and their CEO became our closest partner.

In this way, Huawei and I became increasingly recognized and trusted by our customers. I found I could no longer tear myself away from Comoros. As a result, I transferred there permanently, so I wouldn't have to keep coming for business trips. I became Huawei's only Chinese employee based in Comoros. Over the years, I have witnessed three presidential elections there, and I have engaged with six CEOs of one customer in succession. I have remained, despite how customer CEOs come and go.

"Comoros has the best network in the world!"

In 2014, we moved out of our shabby dormitory and rented a spacious and bright new building. We also got a dog in order to guard and protect our home. That's when the story about me, my cook and our dog in Comoros got out and started spreading around the company.

This dog was too aggressive, so we gave it to a local and got another two dogs, a male and a female. We actually did some brainstorming to give them names. Some proposed typical auspicious Chinese names. I was the one who made the final decision on their names: Revenue and Payment Collection. I wanted to use these two names to remind us of the two priorities we need to work on.

Revenue and Payment Collection discussing how to achieve this year's business goals

Interestingly enough, guarded by Revenue and Payment Collection, our business performance in Comoros has seen constant improvements in recent years. In 2016, our team overcame many difficulties and completed the construction of the national backbone transmission network in this small, volcanic island country. This was also the first submarine cable project in Southeast Africa. This project put an end to the isolation of Comoros from the rest of the world, and, since then, it has been closely connected. Because of this project, Comoros was the best-performing country among all small countries Huawei operated in during 2016.

The backbone network could be likened to a highway, and we also wanted to build a 'transportation network' that would cover the whole country and enable everyone in Comoros to connect to the internet, anywhere and at any time. So, we launched the fixed mobile convergence (FMC) network modernization project. After two years of hard work on planning, feasibility study, loan approval and financing agreement signing, the delivery of this project finally got under way at the beginning of 2019. Once the project is completed, 2G, 3G and 4G coverage, as well as fibre-to-the-home (FTTH), will become available throughout the country. In the future, internet access across all of Comoros will be as readily available as in China.

In terms of our relationship with the customer, we not only ensure successful project delivery, but also put ourselves in the customer's shoes to help them earn more profits. For example, we are now using our expertise to provide customers with business and network consulting services in order to help them increase their revenue.

Personally, I can feel the tangible changes Huawei and our communications facilities have brought to Comoros. It has now joined the global village, and people will no longer lose contact with the outside world when they come here. In fact, I can easily make video calls with my family in China, and use the WeChat app any time I want. There are more and more internet users in Comoros. More people are making friends on Facebook, watching videos on YouTube, and even uploading videos they film themselves.

I remember that when I first came here in 2013, most people did not even have a mobile phone. A few had phones, but they were all feature phones. Today, smartphone sales in Comoros are shooting up. I have a local friend who just started using a smartphone. He happily showed it off to me a few days ago, saying, "Comoros has the best network in the world!"

Most importantly, thanks to the improvements in communications, more and more countries and businesses are willing to invest in Comoros. This has greatly facilitated the construction of infrastructure here. For example, electricity and water shortages have been significantly reduced, boosting local economic development. Some time ago, we deployed a 4.5G network here. Afterwards, Comorian government officials proudly announced, on multiple public occasions, that "Comoros is the first Indian Ocean country to have a 4.5G network!" Seeing this reaction from our customers, we felt very proud.

Today, Huawei has become the most popular and respected Chinese company in Comoros. When Huawei encounters difficulties, our customers always immediately stand up to support us, stressing that Huawei is their most trusted partner.

Huawei staff are like mangroves

I have worked in Comoros for over six years. Many people shared the view that I would only be here for a short time, and one of my managers once said that he didn't expect me to stay in Comoros for long due to the harsh conditions. So, I certainly exceeded his expectations.

I have never regretted my decision to come to Comoros. My experiences here have greatly influenced my views on life, and these precious experiences are invaluable to me. I have become more mature, confident, optimistic and tenacious thanks to these experiences.

The Comoros Office has also undergone tremendous changes.

The company has developed a unified logistics service platform here, and employees in Comoros no longer need to worry about their dining or living conditions. The story about me, my cook and our dogs is now a thing of the past. We now have more advanced facilities for employees when they visit customers, and they no longer need to take a pickup truck or a small boat that may capsize during storms. Our team in Comoros is larger, and more Huawei employees are willing to work on these rocky volcanic islands.

In early 2019, the Comoros Office welcomed three millennials who had just graduated from top Chinese universities. They are all based in Comoros with me, and together we serve as 'the customer-centric three' – a customer-facing team comprising three key project roles. In addition, we now also have some experts who have been with Huawei for over a decade, and other Chinese employees come to work with us on business trips. Our office typically has a dozen or so Chinese employees working together. Although we are far away from home, we work and live happily, like a family.

"Can you swim?"

"Can you drive a boat now?"

After I shared my experiences in Comoros, Mr Ren, Huawei's CEO, asked me a few other questions. He said he would visit Comoros some day and that story about me, my cook and our dogs would be about two men, their cook and their dogs.

The starry sky above Comoros

I sincerely encourage other Huawei employees to come work in Comoros. It is a beautiful country, with clear seas, blue skies and gorgeous starry nights. Many types of fruits and vegetables cannot be found in this island country, but tenacious and versatile mangroves grow well here. They grow between rocks, even though there is no fertile soil or fresh water. I think this fits well with the spirit of Huawei's staff. No matter the harsh conditions we face, we will continue to grow and prosper!

Three Big Screens

By Huo Yao

In the Finance building at Huawei's headquarters in Shenzhen, there is a third-floor meeting room unlike any other. One wall is occupied by a screen 7 metres wide and 2 metres high, in front of which sits a large meeting table. Behind this table are several rows of chairs, all facing the screen. It is reminiscent of the command centres you sometimes see in war movies.

The screen is full of figures showing the financial status of over 200 Huawei subsidiaries in the form of pie charts, bar charts, line graphs and more. Different coloured numbers indicate the current status, warnings about projected variances and progress toward targets.

This is the accounting big screen used by Huawei Finance.

On the 28th of every month, the account-closing team gathers before this screen, with their laptops, to take command of account closing worldwide. Global Shared Services Centres (SSCs) use the dashboard to perform account closing 24/7. When the Shenzhen team knocks off at the end of the day, they hand the baton to the Argentina team. Over the course of just five days, Huawei Finance generates more than 9,000 financial reports and 10,000 incentive reports.

Huawei Finance's big screens are not just confined to this accounting big screen. There are other screens with important roles to play in relation to other key finance functions. When the head of Treasury Management starts his business day, the first thing he does is call up the treasury dashboard. As he watches the flow of money, he can see where problems occur and immediately highlight them. Then he can use the screen to contact the relevant managers responsible for the problems. In far-off London, on the intercompany transaction screen, there is a map that displays over 2,500 different 'routes' (transaction pathways) between Huawei subsidiaries worldwide in real time, with accompanying information about the attendant risks.

For Huawei Finance, a big screen is more than just a big screen. These three big screens mentioned are our command centres.

Accounting big screen: Innovation from zero to one

More than just a big screen

The story of the big screen started back at the end of 2016, when Huawei founder and CEO Ren Zhengfei visited Xi'an to see the newly installed big screen of the Global Technical Services (GTS) Department. Zhang Yinchen, head of IT system transformation for Huawei Finance, accompanied Mr Ren on this trip, following the instructions of Huawei's CFO, Meng Wanzhou.

Accounting big screen

Zhang still vividly remembers the first time he saw the GTS big screen, which is 86 metres long and 7.2 metres high, equivalent to 300 combined 80-inch LED screens. Looking at its full length delivers a powerful shock to the senses. The screen is split into several different sections, showing the current status of Huawei's delivery, supply and services projects around the world. The lights continuously flash, change and update themselves.

"One big screen shows all the work of GTS, worldwide!" Mr Ren stood with his hands clasped, listening to the presentation, and quietly asked if anyone from Finance was in the room. When Zhang Yinchen made himself known, Mr Ren turned to him and said, "When we get back, Finance should install one of these!"

Zhang immediately agreed. He could see from Mr Ren's expression that this was no spur-of-the-moment decision. He had clearly thought about it deeply.

When they returned from Xi'an, Zhang went to see Ms Meng. Together, they called the leadership from the financial Centres of Expertise (COEs) and the IT team to talk it over. In that meeting, Ms Meng described some of her ideas for the big screen of Finance. She said, "I don't want Finance's big screen to just show data. If we're going to do this, we have to make it more than that. I want the big screen to be a platform for digital financial processes." Specifically, she shared three thoughts.

First, the big screen should be able to show situations in real time. This would allow our operations and business results to be displayed transparently, as they happen, in Finance's IT systems. It is no good if you only see the temperature of water rising after it is already at 100°C. Financial operations that lag behind business activities simply aren't worth our investment.

Second, the big screen should support action. When we issue a command, the screen should transmit it vertically down and horizontally out, so that we can escape our outdated, layer-by-layer trickle-feed of information from top to bottom. Transmitting commands through many organizational levels is a waste of time, and the message can get distorted.

Finally, the big screen should enable real-time collaboration between multiple regions. It should be linked to Huawei's mobile office system WeLink so that, at the very least, we can use the screen for teleconferences and videoconferences. That way, whenever we see variances in the data, we will be able to immediately identify the person responsible for solving the issue.

The big screen in Finance was a new idea for everyone at the meeting. Ms Meng's suggestions sparked an excited debate, as everyone added their own ideas.

So, from the very beginning, Finance's big screen was set up to be more of a command centre than a screen. It was going to be a platform that enabled digital financial operations.

The 'all-seeing eye'

The first operation we wanted to use the big screen for was accounting. Why accounting? This was another question we had thought long and hard about.

Huawei's business operations span more than 170 different countries and regions, and we have over 200 subsidiaries. This makes it a challenge to complete account closing at the end of every month. Over 2,000 finance staff members in 7 different SSCs contribute to nearly 20,000 different reports, generated over the course of five days. It's an enormous and complex project. So, it was accounting that made the first move in the campaign to develop Finance's command centres.

On 15 March 2017, the accounting big screen project officially got under way. But developing a whole new command centre would be a complicated operation involving new processes, the fit-out of a whole room, an audio and video system, IT hardware and software, and much more. This was the first time that any of us had been involved in such a complex project. We weren't sure where to start. But, of course, to see further, you should stand on the shoulders of giants. So, we got in touch with a team who had already completed a similar project: the GTS big screen team in Xi'an. They were happy to give us the benefit of their experience and their advice.

The accounting process was already running reasonably smoothly in our various IT systems as a result of the big transformation program Finance had already completed – Integrated Financial Services (IFS). This program had already equipped us with several useful IT tools, like our Enterprise Resource Planning (ERP) system and iSee, the financial data system. Now, we needed to re-integrate over 170 different IT systems, and present the massive amounts of data within them on the big screen through all kinds of analyses: by process, by domain, etc.

The IT team worked with the operations team, and together they were able to quickly produce a prototype model. A comprehensive overview of the company's account-closing process appeared on the big screen, and, based on the integration of IT systems, it also incorporated an 'all-seeing eye' that could connect to our operations worldwide.

For example, one of the bar charts on the screen shows the company's revenue over the past three years. Clicking on the 2019 bar takes you into the next-level breakdown, revenue divided by business group (BG). Now click the bar for the Carrier BG's revenue, and you move to the next level again, which is the Carrier BG's revenue by region, and so on. Standing in front of the big screen, you can zoom in to view even the lowest level of operational data. This is the data drill-through function. It takes you from the company's consolidated reports through the BGs and regions to countries, customers, contracts, and right down to the individual invoices. We built in security mechanisms at different levels of data. This means that when an indicator strays outside its normal values and could start affecting our broader operations, the system automatically gives a warning.

In July 2017, after three and a half months, the accounting big screen went online. It was a revolutionary step forward in how we perform account closing at Huawei. The accounting team excitedly reported that with the big screen, there was no more need for endless phone calls and emails back and forth in order to check up on the progress of each activity. Now, each activity was immediately visible on-screen. Any issues, as well as their potential impacts on account closing, were displayed on the screen using a simple red-green colour code. Green: Everything is normal. Red: There's a problem. Now we could truly see everything, along with a perfect vision of the future.

The team gathers in front of the big screen on every account-closing day

Later, we discovered that almost no other company in the world has a financial command centre like Huawei's. This was the first big screen in Huawei Finance. We worked things out as we went along, full of anticipation and expectation, and were able to achieve the 'Zero to One' breakthrough that we needed.

Big screen for intercompany transactions: A movie coming to life

The most beautiful curves

As the accounting big screen was being launched, work on Finance's second big screen – for intercompany transactions – was well under way.

Huawei's work on intercompany transactions involves close to 150 subsidiaries around the world. Finance needed a comprehensive view of all of the connections between them: one diagram that could give a full overview. As with the accounting big screen, the big screen for intercompany transactions integrated many different financial IT tools, and the data resources required were ready and waiting. But how could we display over 2,500 different transaction pathways on a single map?

At first, everyone assumed our transaction map would look just like an airline routing map. If Huawei's subsidiary in Country A bought some products from another Huawei subsidiary in Country B, then we could just connect A and B with a line. That shouldn't be too hard, surely? But as we looked deeper into it, we found that the operations could include an extraordinary range of different intercompany transactions. Between any two subsidiaries, there might be several different types of transactions going on. Therefore, we might end up drawing a dozen or so different lines between countries A and B. How could we keep all these lines separate and clear? This was the question that faced us.

We know that the road
ahead will demand
more innovation …
However long the road
may be, we will tread it,
from end to end.

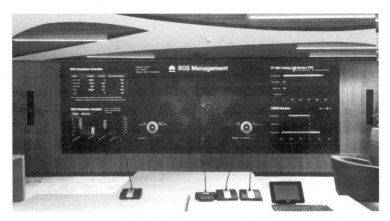

Big screen for intercompany transactions

If you had walked through the project office at that time, you would have seen different configurations of route maps on every screen. Everyone was searching for the right one, but no one managed to find it. In the end, we asked the 2012 Laboratories – a Huawei department responsible for research – for help, and some of their senior researchers joined our team. Together, we carried out a number of technical debates and experiments. One day, we opened discussions at 9 am, and they were still going at 8 o'clock in the evening, without producing any results. Everyone was exhausted, and ready to knock off for the day, when suddenly, from out of nowhere, came a voice: "How about trying Bézier curves?" As soon as this suggestion was out there, it was like a light in the dark. There was instant excitement.

Bézier curves are created using reference points and curved lines. The reference points can be used to drag and shape the curves, which stretch and contract like elastic. With just four points defined on a set of axes, an entire curve can be drawn. Everyone felt that the idea had given new hope to our transaction map. Weary faces started to shine with excitement, and everyone immediately began discussing exactly how it might be done. By 1 o'clock the following morning, a route map that completely avoided the problem of overlapping lines was ready. When the intricate web of Bézier curves spread across the screen, the team saw them as the most beautiful shapes in the world.

Now, on our intercompany transaction map, if you hover your cursor over a certain line, a floating dialogue box pops up to show you the related profit margin. The map gives us a clear and intuitive picture of whether our subsidiaries' operations are fully compliant. The combination of a route map and Bézier curves was also the basis for a successful patent application. Yet, none of us could ever remember exactly who came up with the ingenious idea.

An extraordinary collaboration
In 'The Eve,' the first section of the 2019 Chinese blockbuster film *My People, My Country*, we meet Lin Zhiyuan, the engineer who made the electric flagpole used during the official founding ceremony for the People's Republic of China. The night before the ceremony, he scrambles to complete the installation, solving all kinds of problems to ensure that China's new red flag can fly over Tiananmen Square the following day.

As we watched this part of the movie, we all felt a surge of recognition, because we had experienced our own 'eve.'

When we had started the development of the big screen for intercompany transactions, we assumed that we could simply reproduce the same hardware and software we had used for the accounting big screen. We thought we would just have to repopulate the screen with data about intercompany transactions. However, as soon as we started, we realized it was not going to be that simple.

The first problem was hardware. There was no way to simply 'reproduce' the hardware we had used before. The accounting big screen was in Shenzhen, and we had used a big screen made by a Chinese company. However, the big screen for intercompany transactions was built in Huawei's Finance Risk Control Centre in London, where it could be used directly in their work. After considering the installation process and the need for ongoing operations and maintenance, we chose a screen made by a local vendor in the UK.

The screen relies on a display control system. This is the brain that runs the entire piece of equipment, and would be key to the success of technical planning for the big screen for intercompany transactions. We had already developed a display control system – a good one – during the course of our work with the Chinese vendor when we set up the accounting big screen. Now, we wanted to use that software to control the screen made by the UK company. That way, we would not have to repeat all of the work to create another display control system. In theory, it should have been simple. But it required compatibility between the technical schemas from two competing screen makers.

More annoyingly, we ran into another problem at the same time. Because our schedule was so tight, we would have to complete the physical installation in London and the software R&D in China in parallel. This meant that we would not have time to run verification tests on the London screen before it was set up.

In *My People, My Country*, Lin Zhiyuan was not allowed into Tiananmen Square, so to conduct his own final tests, he built a 1/3-scale replica flagpole. We were not able to go to London, so we went to the Shanghai offices of our UK supplier to conduct our own 'eve' tests. There, we ran a simulation test on the small screen in their testing lab.

Luan Zhuo was the engineer in charge of the display control software, and he led the charge to make this compatibility possible. "It was an extraordinary example of collaboration," he still says today, just as surprised as he was two years ago. "Perhaps it was because we all had good existing relationships, or because of Huawei's excellent reputation, or because everyone believed that we were working on a world's first, and wanted to be a part of it. Whatever the reason, with just a little push from Huawei, the two vendors agreed to work together!"

The plan was that the London screen would be made out of eight 70-inch screens. It would be 1.74 metres high and 6.2 metres wide, with a combined resolution of 7,680 x 2,160 pixels. But the UK company only had two 60-inch screens in their Shanghai lab. The resolution on these screens was low, and they were from a different generation of the technology. That whole month, the Huawei team and both the Chinese and British screen vendors worked closely together on countless simulations and verifications. Eventually, we were able to produce a system that was demonstrably reliable and effective.

Looking back, many of those days blur together, because of the highly repetitive nature of the work. But Luan Zhuo clearly remembers the last time he met with the chief engineer from the UK vendor. He told Luan, "I've supported a lot of customers here in China, but I've never met any who work so hard to resolve every single problem. I really admire you and your team!"

The big screen for intercompany transactions went live in June 2018. The screen shows a map of our intercompany transactions, giving the London team a visual overview of all internal trading. It also has an integrated analytics and decision engine that uses big data and AI to power a trial balance function. This tool enables users to project various outcomes. It is currently tied into subsidiary profitability indicators, so that when a gap opens up between a subsidiary's projected and actual profit margins, the screen displays a warning and offers recommendations and potential solutions. It is a truly helpful assistant that can 'think.'

Treasury big screen: A mobile command centre
Massive clean up

In 2017, as we started developing the big screen for intercompany transactions, we also began development on the third screen: the treasury big screen.

Ms Meng has said more than once that Finance cannot see without data. One of the key functions of our big screens is to bring all of our data together in one place and make it accessible. Finance's IFS program has put most financial processes on a digital footing, producing data that underpins the operations of the big screens. But of the three screens, the treasury big screen depended on relatively underdeveloped IT systems. When we wanted to create a treasury command centre, we first had to abstract and refine the underlying data. This meant doing work on the sources of data and cleansing, converting and integrating data.

Wei Yanran, who had only been at Huawei for a year, was part of the treasury IT team, and she led the charge into the 'data lake.' She has a bachelor's degree in information management and information systems, and a master's degree in finance, so she was very confident in her ability to handle the task.

However, she soon saw that things were not that simple. "It started driving me crazy straight away," she said. "At first, I didn't even know where to find the data, and when I did find it, it came from multiple sources, with inconsistent definitions. It was very low quality." A single Excel spreadsheet might have 60 strings, and each string would require a data search and data mining. Only after this intensive process could the information be added to the data lake. Wei was faced with huge quantities of data, different data definitions, and complex systems and sources.

Treasury big screen

With data, there are never any shortcuts. Wei realized that the only thing to do was work through the mess, so she resolved to get the job done. She would find the data and get it right, even if she had to enter it all into the system by hand!

For example, the main screen would show revenues, payment collection and cash flows. Each of these had one definition used in our financial reports, and another definition used in the incentive reports. The data came from different sources: some from our network business and some from our ICT business. Billing and payment collection data could be found in real time, and in our daily financial reports. Then, of course, there might also be variations between the figures.

Which definitions should we use? Wei listed all of the financial indicators, and each of their definitions, in a multidimensional array. Within each dimension, she collated and compared the information, and then went through it, identifying the differences one by one. She then called meetings with the departments responsible for each set of figures, to discuss how each indicator was used at the company level, by the separate BGs, and in the regions. She gained an understanding of the situations and the processes, and then worked with the responsible departments to pick the definition, standards and data source for each indicator, based on their purposes. There were only a dozen or so financial indicators, so the work looked simple enough from the outside. But it took Wei more than a fortnight of early starts and punishingly late nights to produce the full reference book of finance indicators.

During this period, Wei's roommates asked her: "Why have you been spending so long in the shower lately?" She realized that it was because she was thinking so hard about her data that she had sometimes ended up applying shampoo or shower gel twice without noticing.

Data cleansing was another mammoth task, with nearly 100 people working non-stop simply to mould the data into shape. Everyone was busy collecting data, cleaning it up, tracing data lineage, and then adding it to the data lake. It took more than two months, but the treasury department finally completed data preparation and service packaging. They provided definitions, sources and figures for over 200 different indicators. Over 90 different data services were packaged and delivered, and the main obstacles on the path to a working treasury big screen had been cleared. The full story of that massive effort alone would require many more pages. Within the team we simply say that no shots were fired, but developing the treasury big screen was certainly a battle.

At the end of November 2017, the treasury big screen came online, and the treasury department's working processes were transformed. The treasury managers could now use the big screen every day to control money transfers and flows and manage their capital stock, hedge currencies, etc., in real time. In the past, the Global Daily Reconciliation Centre, which is responsible for final checks of fund security, had to frequently check the progress of reconciliation in each account offline. The centre would also have to contact the relevant staff offline to handle any high-risk issues. Now, they can see how reconciliation is progressing across different regions, sets of books and individual accounts, all on the big screen. During intensive end-of-week and end-of-month operations, the centre can control everything through this single interface, and high-risk issues can be dealt with immediately by calling the relevant staff through the big screen.

From big screens to DMAX

Creating the accounting big screen and the big screen for inter-company transactions were both custom projects. They were high-cost, and took a relatively long time. We needed to think about our future big screen needs, and develop our own technology platform. This would provide the foundation for future big screens, so that we could simply configure and go.

We started developing these capabilities during the development of the treasury big screen. This was another new step for the IT team. Could we learn from others? First, we researched how one of China's online retailers had built the big screen it used during the annual Single's Day online shopping spree on 11 November. But it later became clear that those methods would not work for us. That retailer did everything in a big screen system provided by display technology provider D. All data had to be routed through D's platform, and even if that were possible with Huawei data, the platform was too slow. There was no way it would stand the strain that Finance would place on our systems when we started using our big screens operationally.

If we couldn't use someone else's, we would have to make our own. Liang Liping, one of the IT department's top engineers, held a nine-hour meeting with the big screen project team. Finally, he decided that we would have to develop Huawei's own display system in-house. Once this decision was made, we immediately got to it. Having checked the design principles applied by other companies in the industry, we decided to set up each of the major functions as a separate app. This design meant that several functions that had been set up sequentially would now run in parallel, significantly boosting the speed of the system.

Was there anything else we could optimize? Of course! By changing the format of data requests, we were able to get data pushed to the big screens. This is a little like when you chat online. You send messages to the other person, and their messages pop up on your screen instantly when they reply. This approach ensured that the on-screen data appeared much faster and was always in real time. In fact, our system ended up being at least 20-times faster than that offered by D's platform.

The first time we demonstrated the screen to one of the treasury managers, he couldn't believe what he was seeing. "How can this system be so fast?" he asked. "Is this real data?" We all burst out laughing. We sent someone to check the underlying data, and demonstrated that what the manager was seeing on the screen was the same as the real-time figures. Everyone in the room applauded. "You guys are amazing," the treasury manager proclaimed, and the whole team felt incredible at that moment.

Unlike the accounting big screen and the big screen for inter-company transactions, treasury operations do not require the big screen to be installed in a specific meeting room. Therefore, we decided to turn the treasury big screen into a mobile command centre, so any screen could be made into the treasury big screen through projection. We were able to make that happen using Huawei's WeLink office software. Now, anyone from the treasury department can log in to WeLink on their phone, and put the treasury big screen up on the nearest electronic whiteboard. This allows them to set up their command centre any time, anywhere.

The platform we developed to support the big screens is called DMAX. Today, it has grown to 95 components and 72 modules. It is easily the industry's leading application in terms of mobility and human-screen interactions. DMAX can now also provide a new big screen within one or two days of receiving a request. Any other software platform would take two to three weeks to develop a custom big screen. It's like having our own 'warehouse' that has all the components we need to develop big screens. As soon as we receive a request to develop a new big screen, we just have to find the components in the warehouse and assemble them. When we later put together a big screen for business operations and a compliance big screen, that's how we did it.

DMAX is our magic tool for creating big screens. Now that we have it, more and more big screen projects are getting under way.

Viewing the world through big screens

As of November 2019, Finance had five big screens online. We continue upgrading the screens we have, and develop new ones as required. These screens are key command centres for Finance. We look forward to a future in which they help us stand so tall that we can survey the entire world!

The big screens mean that Finance is no longer a department in the shadows, always one step behind the business teams. Finance is now striding to the fore. Our risk alerts can help ensure that business operations are within the financial safe zone. Our CFO, Ms Meng, likes to talk about making Finance a 'thermometer,' and this is something we are working hard on. We are exploring the mathematics required to build AI models that we hope will make finance management activities like sensitive thermometers. We can then deploy these thermometers within all of Huawei's business operations, so they can take the temperature of the water without interrupting the flow. Finance hopes that this quiet support and monitoring will enable us to promptly keep up with, analyse and alert business operations, and will lead to better decision-making.

In Huawei Finance, when we talk about big screens, we think of flickering numbers, a minute-by-minute record of company operations and an intricate route map of intercompany transactions. We also remember the process of creating these screens: the big cooling fans in the newly-completed Finance building, the puzzlement as we gazed at countless different route maps, spilling out of the office late to gaze up at starry skies, and seeing the first rays of light after working throughout the night. At these moments, all of us at Huawei Finance want to turn to our companions on this journey and exchange words of encouragement: "Amazing work!"

The big screen project was just one small part of the digital transformation of Huawei Finance. That process will be a long and gradual shift. We are just ordinary Huawei staff who are committed to making Huawei Finance digital. We know that the road ahead will demand more innovation. But, however distant the goals may be, we will always reach them. However long the road may be, we will tread it, from end to end.

Cool Technologies for Heat

By Hong Yuping

On the second floor of Building E1, at Huawei's headquarters in Shenzhen, there is a lab that measures less than 400 square metres in size. It is piled high with electronic equipment, both large and small. This lab looks ordinary, and is not particularly well known. However, every year it receives many important visitors from governments and customers around the world. The lab exemplifies Huawei's excellence in basic research and the reliability we build into every piece of equipment. This is Huawei's Thermal Laboratory.

You may be wondering what exactly a thermal laboratory does. To put it in simple terms, it researches how to vent the heat generated by our communications equipment. To ensure the performance and reliability of a piece of communications equipment, good thermal engineering is required to dissipate the heat generated. However, getting rid of excess heat is no easy task, as any doctor who has tried to cool down a feverish patient will know.

I started working as a Huawei thermal engineer straight out of university. In the 19 years since I started, I have witnessed and been a part of numerous thermal engineering projects, ranging from chips and boards to modules, cabinets and even entire base stations. We have worked on cooling for every part of Huawei's product portfolio, based on customer needs, and have helped spread those products around the globe. Along the way, I have seen Huawei's thermal engineering develop in leaps and bounds, from the most basic level to pioneering technologies. I was there as we became one of the world leaders in this field.

Delays costing ¥200,000 a day

Huawei formed its first thermal engineering team in 1999, with just three people, and I was one of them. Our job was to design heat dissipation systems for Huawei products. At that time, it was all about the application of existing technologies. There was no basic research into thermal technologies. As Huawei grew, along with our hardware engineering capabilities, our lack of expertise in thermal engineering started becoming a key bottleneck. The product lines frequently complained about cooling problems.

During a major thermal engineering project for chips in 2005, one of our telecom operator customers asked Huawei to develop a server that integrated four Central Processing Units (CPUs) to support multimedia data processing. The CPUs were made using a 45-nanometre process, which was the most advanced chip technology available at the time.

Chips are the main source of heat within communications equipment. A single powerful processor has a surface area of around just 600 square millimetres, but its heat flux is the same order of magnitude as the core of a nuclear reactor. Channelling that heat away from the chip and out of the equipment has been a longstanding challenge in the telecommunications industry. Back then, we knew it was a challenge that Huawei would inevitably have to grapple with.

At that time, our thinking was simple: more is more! We used fans to cool the chips, so we thought that if we just make the fans bigger, we can cool the chips more effectively. We built the server and tested it. Everything went well until the heat dissipation test that was conducted under the following conditions: high ambient temperature plus single-fan failure. When one fan broke down, the CPUs became overheated and the server went offline.

If we couldn't solve the heat dissipation issue, we couldn't put the server on the market. At this point, every day we delayed was adding ¥200,000 to our R&D costs. We were becoming frantic, and for the next few weeks we dedicated ourselves to finding a solution. We tried many different approaches and dozens of designs for the cooling unit that produced prototypes weighing dozens of kilos. But nothing worked.

With nowhere left to turn, we asked the chip manufacturer for help. One of the manufacturer's most experienced thermal engineers, named Chad, told us that he had never encountered the specific issue we were having. However, he had a very clear understanding of the 45-nanometre chip, and for a full week he worked with us, side by side, as we tracked the changes in chip power and temperature following the failure of a cooling fan. We gradually determined the root cause. With 45-nanometre chips, the chip's power consumption very closely correlates with its temperature. The higher the temperature, the more power is used. That causes a snowball effect; the hotter it is, the more power it draws, making it even hotter. In extreme cases this can cause chip failure. Therefore, an effective cooling solution must consider this kind of abnormal or extreme situation, as well as the accompanying extra power usage. What we needed was not just better cooling, but holistic thermal control for the system.

Eventually, we solved the problem for that chip, but the lesson we learned was an important one. Previously, we had always focused on the problem directly in front of us. We had not looked ahead at what the ever-increasing power of our hardware would mean for future thermal engineering. We had not prepared a stock of technologies to help us stay ahead of the curve. If Huawei was to be a serious player in thermal engineering going forward, we had to understand the latest advances, keep pace with the leaders in the field, and conduct basic research in thermal engineering and its practical applications.

To soar with the eagles, you must first go where the eagles are

In 2006, we began increasing our R&D budget and researching thermal engineering technologies for ourselves. We explored the properties of new fans, heat conductive materials and liquid coolants. At the time, only three of us had worked in thermal engineering for more than five years and could be regarded as 'experienced.' Chi, Xu and I were all sent on missions to Europe and Japan, where there were more experienced workforces in the field of thermal engineering. Our job was to find the right people with the right skills, bring in some top engineers, and build up the team.

Vadim was one of the engineers we found. We asked him to consult for us, and built a whole centre of expertise around him, based in his home country. That team was responsible for researching new thermal engineering technologies, which was the most challenging task of all.

In 2008, the Wireless Network Product Line asked us to develop a new heat exchanger for our customers' outdoor cabinets, which would support the switch from 3G to 4G networks.

We had to enable the equipment to vent far more excess heat without increasing the size of the cabinets or adding more cabinets.

Vadim suggested a new technology that would replace the traditional metal core of the heat exchanger with plastic. Plastic is easier to mould, which would allow us to fashion a more complex shape for the core and ensure a larger surface area for heat exchange. However, if the new shape disrupted the airflow, then the hot air would back up inside the equipment, causing the temperature to rise. Back in 2006, we had done some research in this area with a Japanese company, but none of our prototypes had worked. In fact, they had slowed the rate of cooling.

Vadim ran an experienced eye over our results from that research and said that it was simply a case of reducing the drag. He was supremely confident that his team would be able to make the breakthrough we needed. So, we returned to the Japanese company and started a new round of experimentation.

This international project took three months, with Vadim and his team working in his home country, our Japanese partners working in Japan, and a team including me and a few other engineers working in China. Vadim made the long trip to Japan and talked directly with the engineers there. In China, we used simulation and wind tunnel experiments to determine the drag coefficient of the cabinets. Over the course of several phone conferences with the Japanese team, we worked through the design, defined the product parameters and planned a development timetable.

During the last round of development, we wanted the test environment to be as close as possible to the actual working environment of our customers' equipment, so we shipped our test cabinets from China to Japan. I flew out there twice to calibrate the equipment with the Japanese team. Finally, our joint efforts produced a heat exchanger prototype that had the drag characteristics we required.

Vadim's vision was realized. We had an innovative and environmentally friendly cooling system for outdoor cabinets that was 40% more powerful. It helped us offer the most compact 4G base station equipment on the market. Success always brings people together. At the end of the project, Vadim proposed that he join the Huawei family, so he could dedicate himself to our continued success. He told us that working with Huawei taught him what commitment and teamwork really meant. The thermal engineering team was strong, diverse and had an open way of working. And the company was fast growing and vibrant. Vadim also loves sharing his knowledge and experience with his Chinese colleagues, and today he still often says to me, "Joining Huawei is wise!"

One corner of Huawei's Thermal Laboratory

The strength of a team determines the strength of its technology. Social connections determine the types of talent we can attract, and open collaboration can decide the success of a project. Between 2007 and 2010, we sought out the world's top experts in thermal engineering, and gradually built up centres of expertise in Europe, Japan and other parts of the world. That included hiring around a dozen senior engineers outside China. Our expanded team helped us identify the right areas to focus on, and we started building up a stock of R&D tools. Our research was now keeping pace with the cutting edge of the industry. As a result, our equipment was cooled better than ever before. Our basic research in cooling technologies started bearing fruit, and we were able to catch up to and surpass our competitors in terms of cooling performance.

A fateful encounter with a leaf

As time went on, ICT equipment continued to get more powerful and more compact. This was in line with Moore's Law, which holds that computing will increase in power, and decrease in relative cost, at an exponential pace. For us, the focus of work shifted from cooling single chips to cooling for entire cabinets, along with noise reduction. We had to cool not just indoor units, but also outdoor base stations. The challenges kept on coming.

At the end of 2012, the Wireless Network Product Line once again made a request. This time we had to improve the cooling of the remote radio units (RRUs) that formed part of our distributed base stations.

Huawei was the first company to bring a distributed base station to the market, and it was hugely popular. The RRUs had a fanless natural cooling system, and worked reliably in even the most adverse environments. We had iterated and refined the thermal engineering of the RRUs many times, until we achieved the best thermal performance in the industry.

Following our success, the product team wanted to increase the number of antennas for even better signal coverage, and needed better cooling to achieve this. At this point, there was no easy solution. Every improvement was like shaving 0.01 seconds off the 100 metres world record time: achievable only through rigorous training and incredibly hard work.

We ran a series of simulations to see if we could wring any more performance out of the heat exchanger by adjusting the thickness, spacing, length or angle of the cooling fins. But nothing worked. We felt as though we were at our wit's end.

When you can't solve a problem in-house, it's time to reach out for help. At the start of 2013, we decided to pose the problem as a challenge to the thermal engineering discipline. Our challenge was taken up by Professor Xia, a prodigy with a reputation for thinking outside the box and combining insights from both natural and social sciences.

Even though we knew this project was going to be hard work, it proved to be tougher than we had imagined. We had many meetings with Prof Xia, but the key breakthrough still eluded us. Then, one August afternoon, a young engineer named Tang was walking with Prof Xia around the lake in Huawei's Shanghai Research Centre. As they strolled along, Prof Xia spotted a redwood tree, and started staring at it, as if lost in thought. He then bent down and picked up a fallen leaf. "This leaf," he said with a smile, "might just hold the solution to our problem."

Tang looked at him, nonplussed, so Prof Xia quickly explained: "Leaves absorb sunlight for photosynthesis, so their surface temperature rises. If they didn't dissipate that heat, the leaves would burn. Leaves evaporate large quantities of water to dissipate heat. That cools the surface of the leaf, and keeps the leaf alive. After billions of years of natural selection, all the plants around us today have unique abilities. Your hardware needs cooling just like the plants. We can imagine the outer shell of the cooling unit is like this leaf. If we work out the relationship between the leaf stalk and the veins, we can optimize the design."

This was a moment of inspiration. Evolution is all around us, from the smallest leaf to the largest tree, from patterns found in nature to our social institutions. Beneficial features develop, while useless features drop away. The world we see is the endpoint in a long process of adaptation.

Abstract models and logical theory were Prof Xia's strong suit. We, on the other hand, knew a thing or two about experimentation and applied design. We set about researching the use cases for heat exchangers and the function of each part, discussing which parts needed developing and which were no longer required. After a long process of calculation, a biomimetic design for a heat exchanger emerged, inspired by the cooling principles of living organisms.

One fallen leaf led to a powerful piece of technology. Our innovative biomimetic cooling units were installed in the Huawei RRUs, resulting in a massive 15% improvement in heat dissipation without making the equipment any bulkier. These units also had a harmonious external form factor, making them both effective and attractive. This technological principle was also applied to microwave equipment, micro base stations and other products. It made Huawei products more competitive, and made us the industry leader in miniaturization and high-density cooling.

The breakthrough that made 5G cooling possible

Huawei was determined to lead the fifth generation of mobile technology. In 2014, we began researching multiple-input, multiple-output (MIMO) technology for 5G, which involves using multiple antennas for a better signal. Transmission speeds over 5G would be 100–200 times faster than 4G. The power consumption per bit would also dramatically reduce: 5G equipment would use only 1/100–1/50 of the energy of 4G equipment to transmit one bit. Yet, the total power consumed by a 5G base station would still increase compared to the previous generation. Therefore, discharging the excess heat generated would be vital.

Generally, a heat exchanger has several rows of fins, a bit like a central heating radiator. The heat is conducted from the chip to the fins, which then radiate the heat into the surrounding air. Longer fins radiate more heat, but they lose effectiveness when the length exceeds 60 mm. If you make them too long, the cooling power per unit volume then starts to decrease. The only way to make longer fins more efficient is to make them thicker. However, doubling the thickness of the fins doubles their weight, while the increase in cooling efficiency is only 20%. If you make the equipment too heavy, installation and maintenance become much more labour-intensive. In addition, the iron structures of the cell towers may not be strong enough to support the weight. Cooling, weight and volume: these three parameters were key, all of them sensitive, all of them highly interdependent, and all of them threatened by the demands of 5G.

What could we do to overcome this problem? The central issue was finding how to make our radiating fins more efficient and lighter. My first idea was to use a thermosyphon, which is a closed circuit containing liquid, within each fin. Heat at the core turns the liquid to vapour that carries the heat away to the cool tips of the fins, allowing the heat to dissipate. The vapour then condenses, and gravity pulls the liquid back to the core. This continuous vaporization and condensation would swiftly carry excess heat to the ends of the fins so that it could radiate into the air. We would also reduce weight by replacing our solid fins with hollow structures containing the thermosyphon.

The idea was simple, but in engineering terms it was a tough proposition. Fortunately, I could draw inspiration from real-world experience. When I was a student, I had interned at a refrigerator factory where I had seen how they made something called a 'roll bond evaporator,' as part of the refrigeration mechanism. I wondered if perhaps we could adapt the same technology for our cooling system.

We sprang into action, and immediately set up a four-person team to build a prototype. We started looking for suppliers who could produce the components we wanted. Over the course of a month, a senior thermal engineer named Hui and a senior structural material engineer named Wang toured all of the refrigerator component manufacturers in Guangdong and Jiangsu provinces. They discussed manufacturing technologies, precision manufacturing and cost control with each one. They identified the workers who had the most skill with refrigeration components, and spent a lot of time selecting exactly the right supplier. Within two weeks, the supplier they chose produced a simple prototype of our new design. We called this new technology roll bond cooling, or RBC. Each of the closed pipes contained the same coolant that you would find in a household fridge. When we tested the RBC technology by heating the lower end of the cooling loops, the results were excellent. The temperature remained very even, with a differential of less than 2°C between the two ends.

However, during further testing in the lab, we ran into some problems. Hui steadily increased the temperature along with the power consumption. When the temperature hit 60°C, he suddenly heard a pop. The coolant pipes had deformed and split. The experiment ended in failure.

Everyone started analysing the problem. Was it the refrigerator coolant? The aluminium of the fins? We attacked the problem from both angles and tried to adjust the materials, manufacturing process and quality. Wang worked with other structural material specialists on mechanical simulations, checking if we could optimize the shape of the pipes and toughen the cooling fins. Hui and I looked for new types of coolant to replace the refrigerator coolant.

After a couple of months, however, Hui and I had come up empty-handed, and Wang had only made a few incremental improvements to the structural strength of the fins. We did not have a solution to our problem.

At this very moment, fate intervened. Just as we were wondering what to try next, I went to attend Huawei's Cooling Technology Workshop, held in Japan at the end of 2014. One of the academics at the workshop was describing his research, and mentioned a new type of coolant. My ears immediately pricked up. My instincts told me that this coolant might be a good fit for our project.

After the workshop, I read the relevant reference materials and research papers, and it sounded like the technology might work for us. I quickly conferred with Hui, who was back in China. This new coolant was not commonly available, but we managed to contact a producer, and Hui got hold of a sample. It took another month of testing and tinkering, after which we finally had a thermosyphon system with the thermal characteristics we needed, and that remained stable at high temperatures.

We hoped that we could now build our new cooling fins into the products. But at the end of 2015, there was yet more bad news in store.

Two years of research down the drain?

The specs for 5G MIMO continued evolving, and we discovered that our RBC technology was not going to be powerful enough. In our initial designs, the technology required the chip's heat source to be placed at the bottom of the thermosyphon so that the gravity-assisted unit could circulate. But, the hardware engineers informed us that part of the chip's heat source would be at the middle and upper side of the thermosyphon. This meant we would have to put more liquid into the thermosyphon to absorb the heat from the chip. However, more liquid would block the circulation of the liquid at the bottom of the thermosyphon, greatly affecting RBC cooling performance.

This was a huge blow for everyone in the thermal engineering team. Our design was like our baby, and we had hoped that it would be built into Huawei products to make them more effective. We had spent two years overcoming many hurdles. Surely all of that time hadn't been wasted for nothing? Did we really

As Huawei's founder and CEO Ren Zhengfei said, "We should gaze out at the starry sky and make friends around the world. The more friends we have, the brighter our prospects will be."

have to abandon everything we had achieved? It was almost more than we could bear. I told myself that I should hang in there, and reassured the other members of the team: "We'll find a solution!"

I decided that we needed fresh ideas, and turned to the academic community. I visited several top universities in China, asked their leading professors for help, and worked with them. Professor H was a specialist in phase change for heat transfers, and he had an unusual idea: using an airlift pump as a second driver for circulation, in addition to gravity.

What followed was more than a year of joint R&D. Hui spent 3–4 months on simulation and optimization. In the end, with Professor H's help, we designed a new, patented cooling fin, featuring an airlift pump in addition to the standard gravity-driven thermosyphon. Wang, our structural material engineer, made at least a dozen trips to the supplier's factory, where he worked with their production team to improve the materials and the processes used to make the RBC technology. They made over 800 test pieces before finalizing the best dimensions for the RBC fins, with the correct extrusion process and a low defect rate. Finally, they had a mature fin manufacturing process that was ready for scale production.

It then took the mechanical power environment (MPE) department, the structural material R&D team and our supplier's technology team another year of integration to finalize the design. In 2017, we debuted a light RBC fin that could support the needs of 5G MIMO units. Our design provided 20% more cooling than any other device on the market, or 30% more cooling per kilogram of weight. This revolutionary system was launched alongside our 5G products, leading the market.

Now that we had achieved technological leadership, we were ready to keep it. As well as the cooling system for MIMO, our experience working on liquid cooling systems for electronic equipment was finally paying off. After eight years of hard work, we introduced AI clusters that use Da Vinci architecture at HUAWEI CONNECT in September 2019. These include hybrid liquid cooling techniques that are six times more effective than conventional fan cooling. They will be used across Huawei's cloud product range in the future.

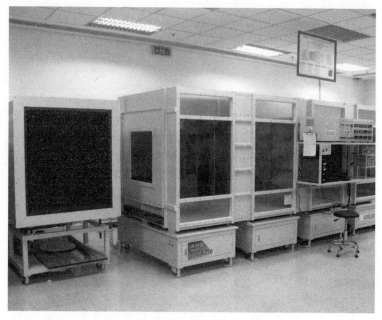

Another section of Huawei's Thermal Laboratory

Over the past 20 years, our thermal engineering team has developed alongside the company, and now has a presence around the world. Our team has grown from three people to over 100, and one-third of our engineers have a PhD. Together, we conduct basic research into the cooling of systems and components, and explore innovative thermal technologies that are high-performance, energy-efficient and environmentally friendly.

As Huawei's founder and CEO Ren Zhengfei said, "We should gaze out at the starry sky and make friends around the world. The more friends we have, the brighter our prospects will be." As one of Huawei's pioneers in conducting basic research, the thermal engineering team stands on the shoulders of giants, and is constantly challenging and surpassing itself. We are always looking for new opportunities, processes and methods to make ongoing improvements.

Thermal engineering has become a key area that helps Huawei remain competitive in hardware performance and maintain its position as an industry leader. At the same time, the open way in which we conduct R&D helps the research world utilize the outcomes of cutting-edge academic research to meet real-world needs. In doing so, Huawei is paving the way for close collaboration between academia and businesses.

The 'Tiger Cubs' of Structural Materials

By Hu Banghong

'Absorb the energy of the universe over a cup of coffee, and take a bucket of glue to stick the world's best brains together.' These words are currently very popular at Huawei. Some say they represent the company's HR philosophy, and they directly apply to me: I am one of the people who was 'glued' to the company. I joined from another Fortune 500 company because Huawei is much more than just a Fortune 500 company.

I have worked as a senior research scientist in the Singapore Agency for Science, Technology and Research, and as an executive in a multinational corporation. I joined Huawei as chief structural materials scientist, and later became director of our Mechanical Technology Laboratory. In 2017, my career hit a new high when I was invited to become a Huawei Fellow. This experience might look like a typical career, but it's not. As I look back on my time here, what makes me happiest is that I have been part of the 'gluing' process that turned the Mechanical Technology Laboratory into one of Huawei's top labs.

'Tiger cubs'

Back during my time as a manager in the Fortune 500 company, my job involved frequent visits to Huawei. I had always been impressed by the grit and dedication of its employees, and believed Huawei to be a great company. After many encounters and much careful thought, I officially accepted a position at Huawei on 14 August 2012, as chief structural materials scientist. This made me the first non-Chinese chief scientist in Huawei's mechanical power environment domain.

I can still remember my first day as if it was yesterday. I walked into the lab to find a 200-square-metre space, with some apparatus and equipment dotted around. There I met with the structural material technology team, which turned out to be made up of a dozen or so inexperienced young staff. The majority of them were only one or two years out of university, and the oldest had just five years' work experience.

This was not exactly what I had imagined. I wondered to myself how I could conduct cutting-edge research into structural materials with a team and lab like this. But I'm an optimistic person, so I tried looking at the situation from another angle. The lab might be small and underequipped, but Huawei was a huge company, and I was an experienced expert. I was confident that we would be able to quickly rise above any weaknesses we had.

In fact, after working with these dozen or so engineers for some time, I quickly found that although they were young, they were committed and intelligent. My team gave me new drive and new hope. Time and again, I have called them the 'tiger cubs' of structural materials.

Building Huawei's own patented material

In August 2012, less than a week after I started, one of the product teams sent us a request. It was an issue that a customer needed resolving, and fast.

This product team selected Material D, which was manufactured to a European standard, because they needed to improve the corrosion resistance of a particular module.

My team and I tested this material, finding that it resisted corrosion reasonably well, but it would often fail to form cleanly in the die. Within a few days, my lab's warnings were vindicated when our supplier announced that they were unable to make Material D into the product we wanted. The date on which our customer expected delivery was drawing closer, and we found ourselves inundated by demands and pleas for help.

I immediately set off for Huizhou, a city about one hour's drive from Shenzhen, taking project engineer Huang and project director Xiao with me. We dived right in at the supplier's foundry, but we were shocked by what we found. The casting die had been newly prepared, but it had gotten stuck after just a single use and could not be removed from the jig. What should we do?

Should we change the alloy mixture? Some of my colleagues were quick to rule out this idea, reminding me that there was a whole process for testing new alloys that would take six months to a year. Moreover, Huawei had developed an approach for solving problems like this – we must find a solution that resolves the main issue, followed by iterated optimization.

We had a problem with our die, so we wondered if the answer was to change the die. One of the supplier's engineers reminded me that creating a new die was generally not a problem, but it would take at least 2–3 months. He also brought up another problem. "Retooling the die is expensive," he said. "It costs hundreds of thousands of yuan!"

That was the situation. But we still had to find a solution and promptly deliver a functional product.

During the Huizhou summer, the temperature inside the foundry was often close to 50°C , so it was like working in a sauna. Now, we found that we couldn't change this, and we couldn't change that, and I felt like a puddle melting onto the floor. Fortunately, with over 20 years of experience, I was able to stay cool. We may have been unable to change the alloy mixture, but we could adjust the proportions of each element in the mix. I could tweak the formula to make the best of a bad lot. I might have been unable to change the die itself, but there was room to improve the injection nozzle and shut-off, where the die and the work piece were actually connected.

Two days later, the foundry called us to say that they had all the materials ready, and were going to start changing the die. I immediately replied: "Don't move, I'll be right there." I grabbed another engineer, Deng, and we drove to Huizhou (as Huawei had a rule that no one was allowed to visit suppliers alone). It was raining heavily, and we weren't familiar with the route. The drive from Bantian, Shenzhen, to the foundry, which normally took an hour, ended up taking us over two hours. Once we arrived, we got straight to work. We worked deep into the night, and figured out the adjustments to the tooling that could get us the right results. Three days later, mass production officially began. Cast alloy components started rolling off the foundry's production line. The components were well formed and free of defects, meaning we could deliver them to our customer. A problem that had plagued us for over a month was finally solved.

A European customer later asked us to deliver better-formed components that were more corrosion-resistant, even in the harshest environments. I worked with Meng, an expert in die casting, to develop a brand-new alloy formula, called D2. This formula used a new method for combining three different metals, and it was drafted into a patent application by a young colleague, Dr Yuan. We quickly began testing the new formula. These tests lasted several months, and involved making hundreds of different components for different Huawei products out of the new alloy. Finally, we were able to measure its properties and determine the exact proportions for the blend to yield the best results.

D2 was a better heat conductor than anything else on the market. It was also several times more resistant to corrosion, and easy to cast. It became one of Huawei's patented materials. Huawei spends billions of yuan on cast alloy components every year, and today all of those components are made of Huawei's own D2 alloy. As a result, our customers are using higher-quality products.

New alloys named after their inventors

2013 was a year of big changes for antennas. Huawei was developing an integrated antenna that supported multiple frequency bands and multiple generations of mobile technology. However, the specifications for the new antenna demanded enormous strength and conductivity, without increasing the weight of the unit. Achieving excellent performance was the responsibility of another department, but minimizing the weight of the unit fell to our structural materials team.

'Reduce the weight' sounds easy enough, but it is extremely difficult in practice. Because the physical structure of an antenna depends on its design functionality, no component can be removed. This means that the only possibility is making improvements to the materials. We had to reduce the weight of our materials, while preserving the functionality, strength, hardness and resilience of the components. To make things even harder, our antennas at that time were already made using lightweight alloys.

So how could we shave more weight off? We would need an entirely new material. We considered an alloy called M, which had long been used in the aerospace, automotive and electronics industries. About 20 years earlier, when I was working in Singapore, I had helped to establish Southeast Asia's first foundry for casting and forming components made of M, so I was very familiar with the material. M was 1/3 lighter than other lightweight materials, but it had some weaknesses; it was much less resistant to corrosion, and its heat conductivity was only half that of other materials. These factors were not a major issue in the aerospace, automotive or electronics industries, but they were key factors for antennas. Some antennas are placed in the wildest terrain and must function reliably for at least 10 years before any maintenance is required. They must also be good heat conductors.

Alloy M was identified as a potential candidate for reducing the weight of antennas. Now, our job was to find ways to remedy this material's two major weaknesses. We knew we would need help, so we prepared Huawei's famous 'glue' in order to stick the world's best brains in the Alloy M domain together. We searched for the universities and companies with the very best track records in working with M. We met with many twists and turns along the way, but eventually found a partner company and worked with them to produce a version of M that had far superior heat conductivity. We then jointly developed a coating for M with another research institute that would make it resistant to corrosion by wind, rain and salt for the required 10 years. We made prototypes and tested them for a proof of concept. These tests confirmed that we had achieved the reduction in weight that the product team required.

The new conductive alloy was named Alloy XF, after the names of the two lead engineers on the project, Xiao and Fu. The corrosion-resistant coating was given the name MW, similarly after the lead engineers Mu and Wang. We later developed another coating used for antenna connections that minimized passive intermodulation (PIM), a measure of interference within the antenna. This coating was named LC after engineers Li and Chen. Within our team, technology is not a cold, tasteless thing. It is a living, human process. This is part of the glue that we use and a form of non-monetary incentive that helps hold our team together.

The scratch-proof phone

You may remember seeing a photo of Richard Yu, CEO of Huawei's Consumer Business Group, with a phone in his left hand and knife in his right hand, using the knife to scrape at the screen. This photo was part of the launch of a special sapphire glass edition of the HUAWEI P7 smartphone in 2014. I still feel pride whenever I see that photo, because that scratch-proof sapphire glass was developed by the structural materials team.

Sapphire glass became the latest must-have in the mobile phone industry at that time because of its strength and attractive appearance. Our competitors had long desired to use sapphire glass, but it was extremely difficult to work with, and the most anyone had previously achieved was using it for buttons and the lens cover. Nobody had managed to use it for an entire screen. The difficulty was that although sapphire glass is very hard, it is also very brittle. Therefore, when it is manufactured in large sheets, it is prone to cracking.

Wait or proceed? We had argued over this material internally. This was a key moment for Huawei phones, as sales exploded. We were brimming with confidence, so we decided to go for it. We would achieve what others could not, and bring another level of uniqueness to Huawei phones. At this point I should specially thank the managers in the mechanical power environment domain. Their committed support was a huge factor in the success of this project.

Research, analysis, more research, more analysis. After going over and over the dozens of different processes that go into the manufacture of sapphire glass, we finally identified the source of its brittleness. The cutting of sapphire glass sheets leaves tiny fracture patterns along the edge, invisible to the human eye. Cutting the glass also generates heat, which extended beyond the edge and into the body of the glass, in turn causing material expansion and opening up the cracks further. Preventing these cracks would require a new technology that could minimize the mechanical damage at the edge during cutting, and avoid excess heat.

During our search for such a technology, we opened ourselves up, and tried sticking more brilliant minds together with a bucket of glue. We carried out wide-ranging talks with eminent scientists and corporate chief technology officers (CTOs), and one new technology stood out: picosecond laser cutting. This method uses pulses of laser light to cut materials, with each pulse being just a few picoseconds long.

You may not know how long a picosecond is. It is one trillionth of a second (10^{-12}). A laser pulse of just a few picoseconds can cut through sapphire glass without generating heat. This prevents the glass from expanding, so no stress fractures are generated.

However, picosecond laser cutting is a high-precision process that requires the careful setting of process specifications, including the frequency and power of the laser, the length of the pulses, and the movement of the piece. We worked around the clock to determine these specifications. Our engineers Lyu and Cai worked in the foundry for almost two months. Eventually, we were able to nail down the process for cutting sapphire glass screens. When the first sapphire glass phone hit the market, it stunned the entire industry.

The 'tiger cubs' have grown up

As I said before, when I first took over the Mechanical Technology Laboratory, I had a young team, with most of the members just 1–2 years out of university, whom I'd nicknamed the 'tiger cubs.' I wanted them to expand their horizons, improve their technical skills and absorb more energy from the industry, so I would always encourage them to get out there and 'have a cup of coffee' with the leaders in our industry. This way, we could build a bigger circle of friends and tap into the wisdom of the wider world. For example, in 2016, we held the Huawei Structural Technology Summit in Yokohama, Japan. The invited speakers included Nobel Prize winners, many eminent scientists, and CTOs from some of the world's leading companies. That event broadened our horizons and helped us identify several potential collaboration projects for the future.

Those 'tiger cubs' have now grown up to become leaders in the field of structural materials. The team is 40-strong, half with PhDs, and made up of senior and mid-level experts. We have generated nearly 100 patents, and have engaged in more than 20 major technological partnerships with leading industry partners. We have been awarded the Huawei Team Gold Medal Award and many other internal prizes. Many of Huawei's Chinese and international customers take the time to stop by the Mechanical Technology Laboratory during visits to Huawei. Here, they get a sneak peek of Huawei's core technical expertise.

"Absorb the energy of the universe over a cup of coffee, and take a bucket of glue to stick the world's best brains together."

Warming the Hearts of Cold Optical Fibres

By Yang Haibin

My name is Yang Haibin, and I'm one of Huawei's 'old-timers' who works in manufacturing. I have been at Huawei for 19 years, but have never spent a day in our frontline sales offices. I work on the production lines, providing the tools that those in sales need to do their magic. But I know that I play my own small part in every victory we win on the front lines.

Part 1: Trapped in a web of optical fibres
Productivity: 1 unit per morning

I started at Huawei back in 2000. At that time, I was a complete beginner with very little experience. The company sent me to the wavelength division multiplexing (WDM) trial production workshop, where I was shocked by the huge Huawei cabinets. My previous company made VCD and DVD players and learning devices. These were small items and, by comparison, Huawei's 2-metre-high cabinets were monsters. Within the belly of these beasts were many separate boards, with thousands of optical fibre cables sprouting in every direction.

What on earth were they all for? My mentor, Zeng, and a colleague called Chen explained all of the apparatus to me, step by step. There were many different parts to a cabinet, but all supported the reception, relay and transmission of communications signals. Every second, hundreds of gigabits of data streamed through the boards, carrying voice calls, data and videos. The signals flowed through optical fibre cables to their destinations thousands of kilometres away, taking information to every home and every individual.

I felt excited when thinking about how my loved ones would be able to make calls to each other, their voices streaming through equipment that I had put together with my own hands. When I went home for Chinese New Year, I would tell them all about it, and perhaps they'd be excited, too. This was a rare opportunity for me, and I was determined to do this job well.

The company started me out with coiling and connecting optical fibre cables in the cabinets. It looked simple, but it was both laborious and time-consuming. On a simple board, there are dozens of optical cables that are twisted together. They have to be separated out, individually coiled, and then lined up and plugged into the correct ports.

I remember very clearly that one day, less than a month after I had started, my mentor brought over a stack of boards, each with twenty or so optical fibre cables attached. Each cable was not much thicker than a hair and had to be individually coiled on a board smaller than a piece of A4 paper. I couldn't even figure out how to get started.

Once I finally got going, I realized that the torture had only just begun. Optical fibre cables are very springy, and they won't just stay where you want them. They are prone to suddenly flexing out straight without any warning. Just as you're in the middle of winding new cables, the ones you've already positioned can pop out of position, messing up the whole board. It's a job that demands deep reserves of patience. When you are just starting out, you don't have a feel for the cables. If you treat them too gently, they won't uncoil smoothly, so you have to reposition them when connecting them to the ports. If you pull them too hard, the thin strip can simply snap. There is no margin for error.

On my first attempt, I felt like a monkey at a typewriter. I did occasionally get it right, but more by luck than skill. By the end of the morning, I had only managed to coil the cables for one board. I was very frustrated by my slowness. This was the first task I had been given in my new job, and I was not doing it well. At this rate, I thought the company might fire me at any time. If that happened, how could I even hold my head up when I went home to see my family for Chinese New Year?

How could I speed up the process? I couldn't see any smart solution to the problem, so I simply had to persist and become successful through lots and lots of practice. My colleagues all liked doing the easy boards, where you just had to tighten some screws. I made it my mission to volunteer for all the fibre boards I could. I practised as I worked. Gradually, I started becoming more confident with the delicate strands of fibre. My coiled boards also started looking much tidier.

However, none of us achieved the kind of speeds we were hoping for. At the time, our throughput was not terribly high, so we were able to keep up, but if we were ever hit with a particularly urgent order, what would we do? We would be in big trouble.

All hands to the pump, even R&D

The crisis we feared eventually hit in May 2003. Huawei was one of the first vendors in China to produce WDM communications equipment, and our market share was rapidly growing. The capacity of our WDM equipment started out at 320 gigabits, but quickly expanded to 1,600 gigabits, and we received large orders for the BWS 1600G unit. Competition for the equipment was intense, and our customers were telling sales staff that they would give their orders to whomever could get the equipment to them first.

The sales teams spent their time with the customers, developing proposals and snapping up orders. Every day they would send orders back to us in production, calling for more stock and more support. However, the speed at which we could coil optical fibre cables was still a major limitation for us. When your frontline teams are calling for supplies, and you have nothing to give them, what will they do?

Some of our salespeople came to the production lines themselves to spur us on: faster, faster, faster still! Others had put orders in months beforehand, all because they wanted to get their hands on the products sooner.

When the pressure was really on, even the R&D team put down their work and came to help us with connecting and testing optical fibre cables. But coiling cables is a job that requires certain skills. It's not something that anyone can just roll up their sleeves and have a go at, and the R&D staff were not particularly nimble-fingered. Many of the colleagues who came to help ended up snapping cables. In the end, they were treating the cables like precious antiques, to be admired from a distance but not to be touched.

Our scheduling staff had to send messages to the sales teams: "Just another day or two ... just another day or two." The product managers would send stern warnings back to our production director: "The deliveries must be ready tomorrow!" We never stopped working, but one person can only do so much in a single day, and our output of coiled fibre boards remained worryingly low. The orders kept flooding in, and the pile of boards waiting to be coiled and connected kept getting higher.

Our frontline teams in the marketplace had done their jobs. Surely we couldn't leave them unsupported.

Combing out the cables

How could we speed up the production of boards with fibre connections? Everyone in the production team became obsessed with this problem. Every day, after finishing as much as I could, I would grab a few old boards and a few dozen fibre cables, and test out every different way of coiling and arranging the cables on the boards: clockwise, counterclockwise, up and down, big loops and little loops. Nothing seemed to make the process any faster.

I couldn't think about anything else. I thought about coiling cables as I walked, as I commuted, as I ate, and when I got home and collapsed on my sofa. My eyes would be staring at the TV, but my mind was only focused on the coiling problem. I even dreamed about coiling. Looking back at it now, I realize this was the time I knew what it meant to be a professional.

After countless attempts, the arrangements, processes and details of the boards and their cables became deeply engraved into my mind, and it was that familiarity that ultimately led to a breakthrough. At the crucial moment, my girlfriend proved to be a key factor.

Yang using the cable comb

She was combing her hair one day as she chatted with me, running the comb through her hair two times, three times, and then twisting the hair up in a coil, fixing it with a hair tie, and inserting a hair clip to hold it in place. She never even looked in the mirror, and built an elegant coil that sat tightly on the back of her head with smooth, practiced movements.

At that moment, the idea hit me: why couldn't I make a comb for my optical cables? When I got into work, I found a piece of cardboard and tried to make my first comb. Of course, the cable comb needed to be different from a hair comb. I had to consider different coils of cables: large loops, small loops and figure-eights. I also needed clips that could hold the cables down as I combed them out.

After numerous failed attempts, I continued trying to make this comb, but just kept failing. It was as though there was some kind of natural law that I had to fail. I still clung to the belief that I could succeed – not because I had some sort of sixth sense about these things, but because of the experience I had gained, and because I had thought everything through clearly in my mind.

Over and over, I kept trying for almost an entire day. Finally, I made a comb that worked. I took it down to the production line, asked my colleagues to try it out, and hey presto! Cable coiling was suddenly easy to complete, and much faster! And because the shape of the comb was fixed, there was no danger of forcing the cables into too tight a curve and snapping them. This was a major success!

There were a number of different boards, so I made some changes to the comb, and was finally able to make a universal cable comb that could work on all different types of boards. With this new tool, we just had to comb the cables out and fix them in place. Our speed increased by over 80%. I then called everyone together and trained them on how to avoid snapping the cables. That increased our first pass yield – the number of pieces you get right first time – by 30%. Everyone said that this was the perfect outcome from combining training with on-the-job experience.

Now, the production team was capable of delivering the goods to our sales teams much more quickly. With this support, our sales teams were able to step out and open up new markets and new territories. The orders kept on flooding in.

Thanks to our timely shipments, one of our sales staff in Xinjiang won a huge order. When that sales employee took us all to dinner and heard about the story behind the cable comb, he joked that it was lucky I wasn't one of Huawei's famous single men. He even gave me a comb carved specially from the finest Xinjiang bull horn, so that I could present it to my girlfriend.

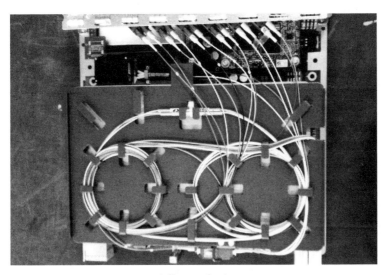

A fibre spool unit

Joking aside, everyone understood that these flashes of inspiration always came from years of experience and deep knowledge of your job. One little bit of inspiration comes from buckets of sweat.

That girlfriend has now been my wife for many years, and the Xinjiang comb is still in my house to this day. The cable comb that was essential to our contributions to the company was further optimized by R&D, and was finally attached to the boards. It now has a technical name: fibre spool unit.

Part 2: Counting the legs of a millipede

Carving from a grain of rice

Nine years after I joined Huawei, a new product freed us from ever worrying about coiling or snapping optical fibre cables again.

This was the Photonic Integrated Device, or PID, which enables much quicker and simpler networking, as well as the much higher-capacity networks required by today's customers. The PID is extremely powerful, combining dozens of different modules that previously all had to be connected with optical fibre cables. The PID chip is like a data superhighway, and every port is like an on-ramp or an off-ramp.

This key technology was designed by a renowned optical transmission expert, who was hired by Huawei to work with the rest of the R&D team. It made me feel great that I was now building a device that used Huawei's proprietary technology with my own hands.

When I saw the very first working PID chip, I noticed it was a rectangular object, three sides of which had long legs sprouting from them. It looked a little like a millipede. On the fourth side, there was a single integrated optical fibre cable.

Under ideal conditions, the PID chip would be directly installed on the board. However, chips are complex creations, and at that time the PID chip was too sensitive to be added when the board was constructed. Therefore, it had to be soldered on by hand.

Each of the tightly packed legs had to be soldered on, one by one. To make things more difficult, the solder beads couldn't touch, or they would create a short circuit. In addition, the beads had to be firm. This process required an extraordinarily steady hand. It was like trying to carve something from a grain of rice. Only those with serious soldering skills were able to do it. This wasn't something a worker on a production line would be able to take care of; it required an artist. Everyone who saw the new product and the amount of work it would require responded with shock, with many saying it couldn't be done.

I wanted to give it a try. On my first attempt, I carefully soldered each leg into place, but of course the chip did not work. It wasn't until my third attempt that I was successful, and no one else was having any more luck than I was. We made an initial estimate that this process would be successful only about 70% of the time.

Even more frustratingly, the new product was cutting edge, so no one in the world had solutions to this problem yet. We had something amazing. Now, we just had to figure out how to wrap it up and present it to the world.

Performing 'surgery' under a microscope

Our sales teams were doing excellent work, and they found a customer in the UK who was willing to trial the new product. We went into the breach!

To begin with, we used dummy pieces for practice, and gradually built up our skills. We managed to get our first pass yield up to 85%. But the fact that everything had to be done by hand was a huge obstacle, and we found it impossible to bring that rate up to 100%.

One day, something on TV caught my eye. The news was showing doctors operating on a patient's heart. Under a microscope, even the heart's thinnest blood vessels could be operated on. This made me wonder, couldn't we use the same technique on the pins of a PID chip? We could make a high-powered microscope that allowed us to clearly see the pins of the chip when we were soldering and monitor the quality of the soldering throughout. This would greatly benefit us during both production and quality checks.

R&D liked this idea, and quickly set to work building a microscope that would help us see our work more clearly. However, when we tried it out, we ran into some problems. Every time we completed a weld or checked the legs on a certain side of the chip, we had to move the board so that the legs were in position under the microscope lens. In practice, we found that we were always shifting the board to the wrong position or looking at the wrong leg under the microscope. It was absolute chaos.

Soldering the 'millipede's legs'

Could we find a way to fix the PID chip in position, and only adjust the microscope from one leg to the next? I tried attaching a sliding apparatus, and after a few attempts, it seemed like it might work. When I took this idea back to R&D, they quickly updated their design, and from that point on we no longer had to move the PID chip in the middle of the job.

With the microscope to help, we resolved our soldering problem, and our first pass yield hit the magic 100%. We found that after using the microscope for a while, we got increasingly used to the work, and we were eventually able to discard it completely and still solder without any faults.

Part 3: Plucking a mote from our own eye
Thousands of tests passed, but still one left ...

As time went on, we were continuing to solve one manufacturing difficulty after another. At the same time, our sales teams were out there winning orders from around the world. Huawei equipment proudly sailed across the Pacific, and we even started receiving orders from Japan and South Korea – countries that are known to be fanatical about quality.

Before customers bought Huawei equipment, they would perform factory acceptance tests at our manufacturing facility. But we found that Japanese and South Korean customers have extremely strict requirements for these tests. We sometimes felt as though they weren't actually performing tests, but instead actively working to find faults with our equipment.

If the factory acceptance tests turned up any problems, the customer would lose confidence in the quality of our products, and all of the hard work done by the sales team would be for nothing. So, we were always incredibly careful with every test. We would think through every stage of the test, and ensure everything was immaculate so that we didn't cause an upset when the deal was so close to being closed.

2010 marked my 10th year at Huawei. That year, one of our new products found a buyer in Japan and, as usual, the Japanese customer asked to carry out a full function test on the new equipment, emulating the configuration that they wanted for their network. More than 100 sets of equipment were to be tested, each of which had to be checked against more than 40 indicators. We also printed out the requirements for factory acceptance tests put forward by the Japanese customer. It was over 100 pages long.

Once again, we knew we had to scramble, but we were not too worried. By this point, the production team was very experienced and knowledgeable. Over the past decade, we had solved many problems and built many new products. We believed that we could tackle this new challenge.

We first simulated the tests that the customer would run, creating the test environment as specified, and started to check one indicator after another. For a while, everything went extremely well. Our equipment was hitting every target, and we all started to relax. We got to the final item on the tests – the temperature cycle test. Once that was passed, we would have successfully completed the test drill.

But, of course, in a twist, after thousands of indicators had been successfully passed ... this last indicator did not hit the required target. During the test, one of the test rigs that had been functioning perfectly for hours suddenly displayed an error message. However, this was only for a second. All of the boards continued functioning normally after the error, and the warning lights did not come on again. The instrument that flashed up the warning didn't show any other signs of an issue. The only thing we saw from then on was the steady transmission of data.

There was clearly some sort of minor fault somewhere, but if we ran the test another 10 times, the same error might never occur, and we knew we might still pass the test with ease. We also predicted that finding the cause of that minor problem would be exceedingly complicated, because there are thousands of ways a fault can be generated. It could be the tiniest thing, like unsteady voltage, a speck of dirt on an optical fibre cable, or a fibre connection that wasn't perfectly set.

Were we really going to put ourselves through all that hassle?

The most beautiful sound in the world

We recognized that if we didn't tackle the problem ourselves, we might end up causing trouble for the company and the customer. Our sales teams were out there working so hard; surely we couldn't let them down.

No matter what it took, we were going to find the root cause of that error. When you are trying to identify the cause of a fault, the most important step is reproducing the fault. Then, you can analyse where it is coming from. It could be a flaw in the design process, imprecise parameters, or a problem with the test environment. All of these were possibilities, and we didn't yet know where to start.

We didn't have many tools at our disposal for fault diagnosis back then. We could check the test logs, and then we had to try and reproduce the problem. First, we checked the error logs, but we couldn't get much additional information from them. They wouldn't tell us where the problem started. My experience led me to suspect that the most likely source of the problem was a lack of redundancy in the design process.

But with so many different boards, how could we identify the culprit? After talking with R&D, I decided to alter the conditions of the stress test. I would make the high temperatures higher and the low temperatures lower, and then keep cycling the test to see if I could force the error to appear again. I also decided to test the network in sections, which would make it easier to find the problem when it did reappear. I tested each section very carefully, several times over, before accepting that it passed.

The temperature cycle test lab was generating a lot of heat, and was closed off. I had to wear anti-static overalls whenever I went in there, so I was drenched in sweat. Each piece of the equipment was buzzing loudly, and this, in combination with the heat, left me nauseous after spending some time in the lab. However, I remained determined to ensure that our products achieved perfection. I watched every indicator light, barely blinking, determined not to miss the fault when it occurred again.

I spent a week in the lab on this, staring at the equipment for more than 10 hours per day. Even when I went to bed, those flashing indicator lights danced in front of my eyes, and the thunder of the equipment fans reverberated in my skull.

On the eighth day, there was a sudden 'dink' sound, and there it was: our phantom fault had reappeared! To me, it was the most beautiful sound in the world.

Now that we had reproduced the problem, we immediately got our colleagues from R&D to analyse it. We found that there was indeed a lack of redundancy in the design process. Therefore, we adjusted the time sequence of the product, and carried on with our temperature cycle testing. We never saw the fault again.

When the Japanese customer performed the formal factory acceptance test, the quality and performance of the Huawei products deeply impressed them. As I watched the customer sign off on the test report, I almost thought I saw those flashing lights again, in a victory celebration.

Conclusion

It is hard to believe that I've worked at Huawei for 19 years. The company has been an integral part of my youth, my ambitions and my hard work. Looking to the future, I hope that Huawei will remain a part of my life. No complaints, and no regrets!

Keep Trying Until You Succeed

By Chen Shuai, Xu Chaofei and Zhu Jinwei

Editor's Note:
In March 2018, Huawei's Executive Management Team (EMT) – the company's most senior
leadership team – added a special item, a 20-Minute Sharing Session, to the agenda of EMT
meetings. During the first session, three cross-disciplinary engineers from the Beijing Research
Centre were invited to share their stories. They appear below.

A Small Boat's AI Journey

"Shuai, the Hardware Engineering Department has set up an AI Technology Application Department. They're in urgent need of AI professionals. Would you like to give it a shot?" My manager asked me this question at the beginning of 2017. At the time, I had just completed my six-month probationary period with the company, and received a very positive evaluation. I was preparing to flex my muscles in the phone-testing department.

Should I give it a try?

Youth represents unlimited possibilities

I remember what my student advisor frequently told me while I was studying at the University of Southern California. "Young people are like small boats that continually go adventuring on vast oceans," he said. "You can choose from limitless directions, which mean countless possibilities. You have what it takes to go through trial and error, and you just need to go out and try. This can enrich both your experience and your knowledge."

So, I thought that as I was still very young, why not give it a go? Even if I was unsuccessful, I could just start afresh. I submitted my résumé, and was given an opportunity for an interview.

The interviewers were very straightforward with their questions. "Our team is a little like a startup within the company, and we want people who are truly capable," one of them said. "You are still a new employee, and your background is in Wi-Fi technology. Do you think you are ready for this?"

All disciplines are actually interconnected in one way or another. What I truly learned from my long school days was not expertise in a given domain, but different methodologies and approaches for analysing and resolving problems. So I replied, brimming with confidence, "I am convinced I can handle it. My job grade does not represent my abilities. AI is a new domain in our smartphone business, and there will be many senior experts to learn from."

I was lucky enough to become one of the six members of the startup team, possibly just because I had displayed such incredible confidence.

A difficult task for two newbies

I didn't have any solid AI knowledge, so as soon as I reported for duty at my new department I started to cram in as much studying on the subject as I could. During the day, I would study the various learning materials stored on our department's server. I looked at summaries left by other colleagues, and asked senior employees to help me analyse the structures of different code. At night, I immersed myself in numerous university courses on the internet, and I studied open courses about AI algorithms from prestigious universities like Stanford and MIT. After studying like crazy, day and night, for two months, I finally got started with AI.

To deliver better smartphone photography, our department planned to implement algorithms for image super-resolution, semantic segmentation and other related features. They also wanted to embed these into our HUAWEI Mate 10 smartphone, which was due to be launched in the second half of 2017. My colleague Zhang Yunchao and I were tasked with image super-resolution algorithms.

I had just gotten started with AI, and Yunchao, who held a doctorate, had recently been transferred from the standards and patents team. He was not that experienced in AI, either. Few companies in China would dare to assign two newbies to take full charge of an entirely new domain, but Huawei is one of the exceptions. I said to myself that since the company had offered me this chance, there was no reason not to give it a go.

I'd like to briefly introduce the algorithm we were working on. It was an algorithm for improving and upscaling small, low-resolution images into bigger, higher-resolution images. Our goal was to achieve images that were both sharp and clear despite a 2x digital zoom. Taking pictures with traditional digital zoom results in a great loss of sharpness. So, what would happen if we used deep learning, a mainstream AI algorithm, to constantly train the model? Theoretically, we could minimize the loss of sharpness when images were enlarged.

Although this sounded simple enough, in practice it was anything but. There were two major challenges. The first was speed. Smartphones usually have fairly low computing power. With the limited computing resources of our smartphones, how could we use a digital zoom and produce images in real time? The academic world already had some methods for improving resolution, but these were slow to produce the images. The other major challenge was how to embed zoom, magnification, denoising, sharpening and other features into a single AI model. In other words, when we took a picture from a distance, we needed to ensure that the details captured were clear even after we enlarged the picture. But almost no mobile phones in the industry had this capability at that time.

Running into dead ends

I knew that fighting alone wouldn't work, and just as our founder and CEO Ren Zhengfei said, "We should absorb the energy of the universe over a cup of coffee." We learned from experts at Huawei's research centres outside China, as well as outside experts and teams, including university professors and experts from leading research institutes.

I was incredibly excited by the company's extensive network of resources and its international platform. I have always been a people-person, so I proactively reached out to related experts and academics, and consulted with them with an open mind. I tried my best to seize every opportunity to learn and improve.

In the first half of 2017, we found that colleagues in other departments were also interested in doing research in this field. So, we set up a project team, with experts from Huawei's Russia Research Centre and professors from a renowned university, and immediately started development.

AI algorithms are mainly about training to ensure better control. An algorithm may be beneficial in one scenario, but make things worse in another. For example, when an AI algorithm helps optimize text within a picture, some details related to nature in the picture may look worse. These kinds of discrepancies require repeated training and adjustments. The problem was that we were not sure if such things would influence each other.

None of us had any experience in this field, and things got really tough. Sometimes we would get stuck on a single issue for weeks. We couldn't see even a glimmer of hope. Gradually, some of the members quit, but Yunchao and I always persisted. We never considered giving up, nor did we want to do so, as we had been working on this project, day and night, for half a year. So we continued, spending over 10 hours each day researching how to improve image quality with deep learning algorithms.

After struggling for another half a month, we finally made some progress – the image quality improved slightly. We felt as though we could finally draw a breath and continue down this path. However, it turned out that if we chose to work in this direction, we would need to research tens of thousands of models. This would take a long time, making it impossible for us to implement the algorithm on time. This ember of hope we had managed to bring to life was extinguished.

Why was everything so difficult? I felt quite upset, and it seemed like the work we were doing every day was useless.

Just keep trying until you succeed

Whenever you think you have reached a dead end, fate makes you believe that you could turn a corner. One day, we were holding a discussion with professors from the university, and it suddenly occurred to me that a new approach to camera zoom data modelling could significantly improve image quality. We looked into this approach and discovered it was feasible.

However, implementation didn't go as smoothly as we had hoped. About a month prior to the launch of the HUAWEI Mate 10, we still hadn't met the requirements – producing images quickly and ensuring there were no flaws in the details. We became frustrated, and racked our brains trying to come up with a solution … but we failed.

At this critical moment, an expert from Huawei's Russia Research Centre suggested that we try another direction. We even invited this expert to Beijing, so we could work together more effectively and push for a breakthrough. With his fantastic support, we made huge progress, and were finally able to produce a demo for image super-resolution algorithms, which ensured crystal-clear text even after a 3x digital zoom. We built this algorithm into our HUAWEI Mate 10 smartphone. Its industry-leading high-quality photography became a key selling point.

On the day the HUAWEI Mate 10 was introduced, I watched the live broadcast of the launch event at home. After that, I even played the piano, something I often do when I am excited. Sometimes I think it was those countless hours spent practising Hanon exercises as a child – piano drills that build dexterity and strength – that taught me the tenacity I bring to my work today. The journey to success does not always make a stirring tale. Often it's simply about thinking harder and trying harder. As long as we persevere, hard work always pays off.

In 2018, we went one step further by improving end-to-end AI fusion algorithms, evolving them from single-frame super-resolution to multi-frame super-resolution. At the time, our phone product line required that we develop a 1–10x digital zoom system. This is like taking a photo 10 metres away from the subject but making it look the same as if it was taken from just one metre away. That was actually very difficult to develop. In the past, we had achieved 3x digital zoom by enlarging a picture with single-frame super-resolution techniques. However, this time, we adopted the multi-frame fusion approach. Simply put, this was not just about enlarging a picture, but about combining seven or eight pictures together into one that could be comprehended by human eyes.

This was a massive challenge, but given my previous experience, I had already braced myself for a difficult challenge. I kept a close eye on industry trends, and conducted analyses and experiments whenever a new academic paper was published. I even developed datasets for multi-frame super-resolution, and conducted many experiments over and over again to improve my AI training techniques.

Huawei's smartphones combine our company's own hardware and software, giving us huge possibilities to tap into our potential and make improvements. After more than six months of constant efforts, we finally built the industry's best 1–10x digital zoom into our HUAWEI P20 and Mate 20 smartphones.

I feel like I am an amateur surfer who got lucky enough to catch the big wave that is AI. In this emerging industry, I continually have to swim hard; otherwise, I will sink. I know there is still a long way to go, and I have a lot to learn. This new domain requires ongoing innovation, original thinking and creativity. I love what I do, and I believe that those who persevere will always prevail.

Coding Is Another Option

In 2016, I graduated from Tsinghua University, where I had studied in the Department of Chemistry, School of Sciences. I joined Huawei's distributed storage software development team that same year. Many people asked me why I, a chemistry graduate, chose to go into coding. My answer was simple: "I love it."

It feels amazing to run a program and wait for the results

I have been enthusiastic about science ever since I was a little kid. In elementary school, I was really interested in mathematics, during my junior high school years I was obsessed with physics, and in senior high school I participated in numerous chemistry contests. These experiences helped me build a solid knowledge base. At university, I was consistently placed among the top three in my class for chemistry, and was given more freedom and possibilities.

Coding was yet another option in my life.

The first time I encountered coding was during a general course as part of my undergraduate study. While I was waiting for a program to run, I found that I had the same feeling I would get when observing a chemistry experiment. I found this really interesting. Later, I spent almost all of my time after school learning how to code. I worked my way through 10–20 books on the subject and got to the point where I was able to code myself.

I often immerse myself in the things that I love. Some might say that I'm a man of focus, but some of my friends joke that I am as dull as a block of wood. During my graduate study, I became obsessed with the card game Texas Hold 'em, a variant of poker. Finding myself continually rebuffed whenever I invited others to play with me, I developed a program that allowed me to play the game by myself. That same year, I took part in the first Huawei Software Elite Challenge, as the theme of this competition was Texas Hold 'em. For two weeks straight, I would start programming using C++ as soon as I finished my work at the chemical lab. I adjusted the program little by little, and during this process my interest shifted from playing Texas Hold 'em to writing algorithms. My heart was filled with a sense of achievement whenever I successfully tackled a difficult technical problem.

I took part in the competition out of my interest in playing poker, and it had never occurred to me that I would make it into the top 32 and win recognition for my coding skills. Because of my outstanding performance, I was able to skip the technical interview and proceed directly to the subsequent interview process at Huawei. This changed the trajectory of my life, and I made up my mind then and there that I was going to join the company.

I was still in my third year of doctoral study, one year away from graduation, but I was eager to become a coder.

A chemistry student becoming a coder

Many people wondered why a chemistry major would choose to become a coder. Perhaps in the eyes of most people, chemistry is still a traditional discipline, primarily about conducting experiments in labs. In reality, the boundaries between different disciplines have been broken down.

When I was a graduate student, my research area was theoretical and computational chemistry – an emerging discipline that combines chemistry and computer science. Simply put, it's about converting theoretical chemistry formulas into programs, and using simulations to calculate the properties of molecules and how they change over the course of a chemical reaction. This process can help explain or predict various chemical substances and reactions. The discipline is mainly about formula derivation, coding, simulation and calculation, and numerical analysis. Computational chemistry led me to discover the beauty of coding and, having been a student of chemistry for years, I'm meticulous in everything I do.

My department offered me numerous opportunities as soon as I was onboarded at Huawei. However, I felt apprehensive, as I didn't know whether my coding skills would be adequate for the job. After a period of adjustment, I found that coding shared many similarities with chemical experiments. They both require contemplation and careful design, and they both centre around converting certain inputs into outputs. In chemistry, we design chemical formulas and consider the steps of chemical reactions, a process that involves a lot of uncertainty. Before starting chemical reactions, we would develop a detailed design, carefully planning each step and doing everything to control every variable. Even a tiny change could cause completely different experiment results. For example, if an experiment is not carried out precisely, you can end up with a paste instead of the desired crystalloid. In some cases, a tiny misstep could prove to be life threatening.

Seven years of experience in chemical experiments helps generate near-perfect code

The habits and experience from my time as a chemistry major have subtly influenced the way I code. Before I begin to code, I try to predict the functional modules to be developed, the target scenarios that will apply and the use cases I want to design, and then use programming languages to write the code. This way, it is possible to write near-perfect code in one go, and effectively limit any defects.

In 2017, our team was developing a performance-enhancing feature on a product, and I was responsible for this task. In the early stages, I produced a module design, which I tried to make as detailed and comprehensive as possible. I designed over 230 self-verifying use cases for 4,000 lines of code. This was the first time I had ever designed automatic testing for a complete service code path using a new framework. Previously, I had always performed such tests by unit, based on modules. After the development was completed, very few problems were identified by testing staff. My way of working allowed me to maintain an incredibly low defect rate for all the features I had developed, both at the testing and live network stages. The code quality I delivered received recognition from my team members.

In July 2018, I was selected as a member of the company's Task Force. This team consisted of excellent entry-level employees from many different departments. Our team was focused on developing trustworthy software, and engaged with software teams that provide end-to-end support for 5G products. We started a pilot for wireless network products, and built the environment and tools using a normalization approach. Our ultimate goal was to continuously optimize software architecture and gradually resolve a series of long-standing software engineering issues. Before this, I was just focused on the service code for storage products; developing trustworthy software allowed me to see the bigger picture. The more I learned, the more I realized I didn't know. This drove me to keep learning and keep up with changes in the industry.

I chose to become an engineer at Huawei because the work interested me. The company boasts a large platform that offers numerous opportunities and a wealth of possibilities. I've always believed that as long as I work hard and demonstrate my ability, Huawei will always give me the opportunity to realize my value.

Although I chose to hang up the laboratory coat that had accompanied me for seven years, I feel that chemistry has remained a part of me. I hope that the pressure and motivation created by this cross-disciplinary experience will enable me to continually advance up the career ladder.

When Mathematics Meets Code

Mathematics is everywhere, from objects in our homes with different geometric patterns, to getting a task done in the shortest time possible through proper planning, to calculating interest rates for wealth-management products.

Is mathematics really that simple? Not really. It requires intense thinking and reasoning. Take the Poincare Conjecture for example. Numerous scientists racked their brains over this theorem about spatial topography. Some spent their entire lives trying to prove it, but ultimately failed. The Poincare Conjecture was not proven until over a hundred years after it was proposed.

So, what kind of wonderful outcomes can we expect when mathematics, which is simple yet complicated, is applied to code and algorithms?

In 2014, I joined the database development team of the Gauss Laboratory at Huawei's Central Software Institute, after spending nine years as a student of mathematics. My aspiration was simple: to develop a product that benefits everyone.

My doctoral supervisor often said to me, "There are two directions in mathematics: one is from simple to complex, while the other is from complex to simple." To this day, I still benefit from these words.

Simplifying things with mathematical thinking

In November 2015, I took over the research of dynamic compilation techniques for the Low Level Virtual Machine (LLVM). LLVM is a compiler framework designed to optimize programming languages and links during compilation and then generate code, with the goal of improving database queries.

Simply put, I needed to develop a system that could identify user needs and provide customized services based on the characteristics of the individual tasks that users wanted to complete. By analogy, when you buy clothes, either online or in a physical store, you make a lot of choices. But, if you had someone tailoring your clothes for you, it would save you the trouble of choosing the type, size, colour and pattern. In the world of databases, LLVM is like that tailor.

This set of techniques was very complex to use, because we had to combine three different languages – C language, assembly language, and dynamic compilation language. It's like gathering three people who speak Chinese, Russian and English, respectively, and then immediately getting them to understand each other.

Almost everyone on our team said they didn't get it, including me. At the time, I didn't have much knowledge about this, and there were only a few peer companies that were doing research in this field. That left me with limited channels to seek assistance. I believe that God helps those who help themselves. In my father's words, "My son is not particularly smart, but he always works hard." Now that I had been assigned this challenge, I would try to find a solution no matter what.

The modelling thinking I had developed over many years of studying mathematics provided me with another angle to approach the problem. From the perspective of computer engineering, one would start with language conversion, but this was extremely difficult to achieve. For me, these three sets of languages could be abstracted into three mathematical models. Generally speaking, a mathematical model is first about defining basic elements, then summarizing these elements, and forming a set. With this set, we can then define measurement and operation rules, apply theorems, lemmas (citation forms) and propositions, and determine the simplest solution to the problem.

Similarly, for this set of techniques, we had to first break down the syntax for one language set, define the instructions we were going to use, and classify these instructions into different groups. Then we would define operations (addition, subtraction, multiplication and division) and establish a one-to-one mapping relationship between database programs. Here, mapping meant writing programs in different languages, while their corresponding functions remained exactly the same. I would then need to establish equivalence relations between the three sets of languages. Upon seeing the code of the first language set, my brain automatically started to generate the code for the other two languages. Everything was within my grasp.

After two years of hard work, we were able to optimize the dynamic compilation of core execution operators for databases, which improved the performance of key operators several-fold. Huawei successfully launched GaussDB 200, the first domestically produced product in China that supported this function. Today, this product has found application in finance, government, education and other sectors across China. What began as a small aspiration years ago is now a reality.

Safeguarding databases with mathematical argumentation
In 2015, I was also independently responsible for ensuring database security. Back then, this domain was like a vacuum in my project team. To ensure security, we had to deal with attacks against the systems, and also provide effective measures to protect data privacy and prevent information leakage after such attacks occurred. During this process, we had to comply with thousands of security specifications, implementing each and every one of them. But following this process would be too inefficient. Could we think outside the box?

I found that mathematical argumentation could play a key role. The industry had defined security specifications, such as those for identity access and cryptography, which must be implemented based on different modules. However, the underlying logic behind actual service scenarios was different. For example, a user login mechanism may include multiple modules, such as identity access, password and network communications transmission. Therefore, I wondered whether it was possible to develop a security mechanism based on the actual logic behind services.

Following this approach, I developed end-to-end, system-level security capabilities, from secure logins and data protection to security audits. Our version passed the audit of the company's Internal Cyber Security Lab, defect-free, and went on to support Data Warehouse Service (DWS), a cloud-based distributed database service that was commercially deployed by Deutsche Telekom.

Hua Luogeng, a famous Chinese mathematician, once said, "Making complex things simple is the way forward, not making simple things complex." We must simplify complex things. Mathematical argumentation can be used to break down and reorganize specifications. We can then go through necessary argumentation, mapping and modelling, and find the simplest and most logical way to execute a certain service.

Helping top minds grow in areas that interest them

In 2019, I began taking responsibility for setting up the GaussDB security technology team, which was tasked with establishing Huawei's competitiveness in database security.

Our team members came from Huawei's research centres in Beijing, Shenzhen and Shanghai, as well as research centres outside China. Many of them were new employees, including PhDs and other top minds. In the second half of 2019, one of my priorities was to develop them, help them find their areas of interest, determine their best roles and maximize their potential. However, this was not too much of a challenge for me, as I once served as a mentor for new employees with PhD degrees.

Applying the same 'divide and conquer' methodology we use in mathematics, I was able to fully understand their capabilities and adopt differentiated management approaches for each of them. Of course, identifying their areas of interest – and encouraging and helping them to work hard on these areas, and make breakthroughs – was more important than anything else.

Many colleagues say that I am a cross-disciplinary engineer. Strictly speaking, that's not true, as all sciences boil down to mathematics. The beauty of mathematics lies in its ability to turn complexity into simplicity, allowing us to accurately express an engineering problem and think outside the box to solve it. The wonder of mathematics also lies in the fact that it exists in everything around us.

PhD Corps:
Cracking the Toughest Nuts

By Jiang Xiaoyi

If we imagined a person's knowledge as a circle drawn on a blank sheet of paper, we would expand the circle as that person received primary, secondary and college education. However, this starts to change when they study for a doctorate. To reflect this kind of study, we would need to zero in on a specific point within that circle and drill a deep hole into it. This is because obtaining a PhD is all about specialization, and requires incredible perseverance and the relentless pursuit of excellence.

Each PhD holder is like a 'chisel,' capable of carving a unique path. Can you imagine the power of a team comprising dozens of PhDs? When there is a clear way forward, the team heads in that direction with enthusiasm. When there is no clear path, they do everything they can to create one, even through the hardest rock.

At Huawei, we have such a team – the PhD Corps, working on multiple-input multiple-output (MIMO), an antenna technology that is critical to the rollout of 5G networks. Though members of the Corps are distributed among sub-teams in Shanghai, Beijing and Chengdu, all of them focus on one thing and one thing only: multiple-antenna technology, which has been crucial for improving the spectral efficiency and capacity of 5G systems.

The three sub-teams have been dedicated to cracking this tough nut. They have not only proposed a number of original technologies, but also pushed for these technologies to be incorporated into international 5G standards. They have carved out a unique path of their own.

The Shanghai team: Never accept second-best

"We crave challenges. That's why Werewolf, one of the most brain-racking games, is so popular among us. We can literally play the game for days," says Dr Bi Xiaoyan, the leader of the Shanghai team, who joined Huawei's 5G research group right after completing her doctoral education.

When asked to describe the team, she says, "The whole team moves quickly while maintaining its composure. We always dare to align our goals with the best in the industry and never accept second-best."

What's the best way to manage a team of more than 10 PhDs? Bi has found that the most important thing is to assign everyone to the right position so that they can do what they are best at. She says that it is essential to pay attention to each person: introduce some humility when someone becomes complacent after successes; provide encouragement when someone encounters setbacks; and give direction when someone is lost and confused. She follows a 'work hard, play hard' philosophy. This is the climate that shapes the team. In a team like this, inspiration often arrives naturally. For example, the ideas for a 'non-uniform codebook' and a 'three-stage codebook' came, pretty much out of the blue, from two young PhDs.

In 5G systems, the more antennas there are, the larger the capacity is. This is similar to vehicles driving on a road. The more lanes there are, the more vehicles can drive at once. But the challenge lies in working out how each vehicle can drive at an optimal speed, whether it is a truck or a car, and this requires a lot of complex design work.

A codebook functions like a navigation system in a vehicle. When a vehicle is heading to a destination, it relies on the navigation system to plan the optimal route. The more accurate the navigation, the quicker the journey.

Dr Jin Huangping, who obtained his PhD at Tsinghua University, is a reserved individual who loves challenges and always seeks perfection. If you ask him to give 100 percent, he will give you 120 percent. After passing his probation review, Jin's first task was to write codebook simulation code. After analysing the previous codebook, he had a gut feeling that there was a better way to do it. To determine the best solution, he stayed in the lab for a few straight days and nights. In addition to commissioning simulation equipment and working out all kinds of ratios, he would discuss any new ideas he had with his mentor, Shang Peng. You could see bags under the young man's eyes.

"Why work so hard?"

"I just want to find the best solution."

Bi is unsurprised by his obsession with work. "These young PhDs are incredibly driven," she says. "They won't stop until the best solution is found. The most challenging tasks are simply made for them!" That said, her heart aches when she sees her team members work into the wee hours of countless nights.

After numerous simulations and repeated commissioning, Jin was struck by a new idea – a non-uniform codebook.

Imagine a road with five lanes. How can we ensure that the maximum number of vehicles are able to travel along the road each hour? If we set a uniform speed limit of 80 km/h for all lanes, we cannot maximize traffic flow. To increase efficiency, we can reserve certain lanes for certain vehicle types, and set a different speed limit for each lane. For example, truck lanes could have a speed limit of 60 km/h, while car lanes could have a speed limit of 100 km/h.

The non-uniform codebook design is based on a similar principle, applying standards in a non-uniform way to significantly boost codebook performance and accuracy. The non-uniform codebook was quickly incorporated into international standards for 5G after being submitted to the 3rd Generation Partnership Project (3GPP).

The pursuit of excellence didn't stop there. Back then, Dr Wang Xiaohan, who had a PhD in electrical engineering from Tsinghua University, had just joined the MIMO team. This mild-mannered young man didn't talk much and preferred to keep a low profile, but he was reliable and extremely tenacious. As he discussed the codebook design with Jin, some new ideas started to form. After many rounds of calculations and deductions, Wang proposed an advanced version of the design – a three-stage codebook.

If we once again imagine the codebook as a road with five lanes, the purpose of this codebook was to ensure that when the vehicles in the lead sped up, other vehicles behind them would automatically follow suit. This would eliminate the need for routing. Compared with its predecessor, this solution seemed like a recipe for better performance. It still had to be tested, but everyone was incredibly excited and couldn't wait to celebrate the idea over hot pot.

However, during the simulation analyses that followed, one team member pointed out a potential problem. "Despite the potential performance gains, the algorithms we need to develop for this solution would be extremely complex," he suggested. "It wouldn't be worth it."

This comment clearly rained on Wang's parade. He sat away from everyone else, not saying a word. A moment later, he came over, all worked up, and practically shouted, "I'm not convinced!" At that moment, he was no longer the composed young man we had known.

He thought that there must be a way to reduce the complexity of algorithms. Looking through papers and all kinds of research literature, talking to experts and brainstorming with team members,

Wang pored back over the entirety of the previous research process. Eventually, he found a solution – phase correction for feature vectors of different frequency bands. With this correction, the complexity of the new codebook algorithms was significantly reduced, while the performance gains were maintained.

The previous concern turned out to be a false alarm. The codebook solution was well received at a 3GPP conference, and the phase correction algorithms became one of the most popular topics that other companies discussed with Huawei at the event.

The ultimate goal of the codebook design is to achieve the highest Precoding Matrix Indicator (PMI) accuracy, at the lowest possible feedback overhead. This is a road with no end, because every time you reach a milestone, there is another one waiting for you. However, this excites the young team, because 'no end' means they can always find a better solution.

"Every step of the way is difficult," they like to say, "but we persevere in our own way and strive to keep achieving technological breakthroughs."

The Beijing team: Debates are the best route to the truth

The biggest challenge facing the Beijing team was how to make the most of reference signal sequences, and they had been working on it for a long time.

"Is there a traffic jam? Is it raining? A team of scouts can be dispatched to get the answers," says Dr Qu Bingyu from the Beijing team. He's using a road metaphor to explain the team's research.

"The reference signals are our version of scouts, which take the measurements. What if a vehicle deviates from the prescribed route? This is where the reference signal sequence comes into play, with its correction functionality. To some extent, reference signals are like signposts."

Since joining Huawei in 1998, Qu has been delving into the area of reference signals, and has delivered some amazing results. During his 20-plus years with Huawei, he has witnessed an increasing number of the company's proposals become part of international standards for 3G, 4G and 5G. In this process, a large number of key technologies related to reference signal sequences have been incorporated into international standards, playing an important role in Huawei's patent negotiations.

"Long-term efforts lead to breakthroughs," says Qu. "The technical expertise we have built over the years has enabled us to achieve constant breakthroughs. Our achievements have been built on the work of those who came before us."

As an expert in the team, Qu hopes to pass on the technology to younger generations of engineers through coaching.

"It is a noisy, young team, but one that I am happy to be around," he says. Every day, as he steps into the office on the 5th floor of the Huawei building in Beijing, he hears heated debates. When there is any disagreement on a conclusion or hypothesis, one PhD will be scribbling down the deduction process on the whiteboard, with the rest of the team looking on and asking questions. To them, what matters most is the technology.

They believe that the right way to reach a technical consensus is always through technological analysis and verification. The team's technical debates are always intense, with rebuttals being thrown around that border on ruthlessness. But everyone always follows one key principle: objections are always welcome. If objections are reasonable, they can drive improvement. If not, debates will help reveal the truth. "This is exactly what we need – an intense and inspiring environment that allows for open technical discussions," says Qu.

The Beijing team's most recent research project was low Peak-to-Average Power Ratio (PAPR) reference signal sequences. This technology is designed to allow the reference signal – the 'scout' – to detect channel information over long distances at the cost of some accuracy.

Can't you have both? Thanks to years of experience, Qu was keenly aware that although the time domain sequences could reduce the PAPR, the lack of flatness in the frequency domain would reduce performance. Therefore, frequency domain flatness also had to be factored into the design of time domain sequences.

This information was followed by rounds of discussion, design, simulation, results analysis, correction and algorithm optimization. This process continued until optimal performance was realized. After overcoming a series of difficulties, the team found the perfect sequence during a simulation experiment. This sequence not only delivered low PAPR, but also guaranteed frequency domain flatness, as well as low interference between inter-cell sequences. The solution delivered excellent performance in all applicable scenarios.

When talking about this exciting breakthrough, Qu can't hide his joy: "What young people need most is trust. We just need to give them the opportunity to shine!"

On 22 April 2019, the sequence design rule of frequency domain flatness was officially written into the relevant international standards for 5G. Upon hearing the news, even the usually reserved PhDs couldn't help but boast a little:

"Making our mark on the 5G era – now that's something to brag about. When my children grow up, I can proudly tell them that their father takes some of the credit for the pervasive AR applications and 8K movies they are enjoying!"

Many companies that want to carve out a space in the 5G market have made heavy, long-term investments in the key areas of 5G research. Throughout this hard-fought battle, the Beijing team played a major role in defining new standards. For all team members, it was truly a dream come true!

The Chengdu team: A group of young PhDs with no fear

The Chengdu team primarily consists of young PhDs, who are responsible for researching high frequencies related to 5G, as well as developing their standards and conducting prototype verifications. Among the 20 members, over a dozen received PhDs from top universities in the electronic information domain. The average age of these individuals is around 30. Although many of them only recently graduated and have little work experience, they are deeply knowledgeable when it comes to theories and scientific methodologies. More importantly, they have the courage to face challenges head-on and forge ahead. These traits make them a responsive team that is always prepared to fight and win tough battles.

High frequencies had not yet been used in civil mobile communications at scale. If this was to change, many challenges lay ahead. "High frequencies in 5G are like highway tunnels, where the road is very wide," says Dr Zhang Xi, the leader of the Chengdu team and a PhD graduate of the Hong Kong University of Science and

Technology. "What we need to do is promptly find the shortest and fastest route, and smooth the road in the tunnel so that vehicles can move through the tunnel quickly."

"We are like Super Mario," he adds, with a big smile on his face. "We work tirelessly and are undaunted by hardship." Zhang is a very humorous young man and is extremely passionate and logical when it comes to technology.

The tunnel mentioned by Zhang refers to a wireless communications link between a base station and a user device. In contrast to 4G, which works at lower frequencies, the 5G tunnel uses high frequencies and has to be dug from both ends. This sounds like an easy mathematical problem that is just a question of connecting two dots. However, the user device doesn't know where the base station is and the base station doesn't know where the user device is, what the surrounding environment is like, or what changes have happened or will happen. A smart design and close collaboration between the base station and the user device are needed to quickly find the shortest and fastest route. This is a systematic process. In addition, 'roadblocks' must be removed and 'water' needs to be drained. The road has to be smoothed to ensure that vehicles move through the tunnel safely and quickly. All of these problems needed to be addressed by the Chengdu team.

Huawei's Chengdu Research Centre started researching high frequencies back in 2012. Building on this experience, the Chengdu team conducted extensive research and analysis and proposed two technical solutions: beam management and phase noise pilot. These solutions could only enter commercial use after being included as part of international standards for 5G. Zhang attended many standards conferences organized by the 3GPP, but still wasn't making significant progress.

He still remembers the meeting he attended in Prague in October 2017, which was the second-to-last meeting before the first version of 5G standards took shape. He was so nervous that his palms were sweating. He says, "I knew that our chances were going to be incredibly slim if we missed this window of opportunity." When he first faced fierce competition from peer companies, he wasn't sure what to do. However, he relied on his extensive preparations, and after waiting patiently, he seized the opportunity.

This 'battle' of standards is certainly not a one-man fight. Our standards representatives go head-to-head with our competitors in conference rooms, and they have the ongoing, strong support from the research team behind them. Sometimes, there are 20–30 companies submitting hundreds of different proposals. To ensure that Huawei's proposal stands out from the rest, the team at the back office needs to analyse and assess all of the submitted proposals as quickly as possible, understand the pros and cons of each, and then outdo them one by one.

This was the first time that high frequencies for 5G were to be standardized by 3GPP. The formulation of standards is intertwined with the architectural evolution of base stations and devices. They restrain and support each other. The young PhDs had no fear in the face of these challenges. They remained curious and were always prepared to delve deeper into every problem they encountered. They have been instrumental in promoting the standardization of high frequencies for 5G.

Dr Guan Peng, who graduated from Paris-Sud University, organized numerous technical discussions across three different time zones. These discussions aimed to improve technical solutions and increase the competitiveness of our standards. On many nights, he was called into conferences with colleagues from the Wireless Network Product Line, HiSilicon, or the Consumer Business Group to discuss how to realize a solution in accordance with the relevant standards and how to provide devices and pipes that would not be constrained by these standards. All of these efforts aimed to achieve one goal – making Huawei products more competitive.

As high frequencies for 5G were covered during many different sessions at the standards conference, the Chengdu team had to work around the clock in order to align their schedules with concurrent sessions. Eventually, thanks to the much more competitive proposals and well-devised tactics, Huawei was able to win over as many peer companies as possible and managed to get a majority vote on the beam management and phase noise pilot solutions we had proposed. Several of our proposals were included as part of international standards for 5G, and we managed to secure a foothold in this uphill 'battle' of standards.

Whenever they achieve
a goal, they feel an
overwhelming sense of
joy and excitement. In
these moments, they
see that the late nights,
the tears, the detours
and the setbacks were
not for nothing.

Making a difference with like-minded partners

At Huawei, the PhD Corps finds its value by bringing together members from different teams to establish lean, elite teams that can crack the toughest nuts – making quick breakthroughs and helping Huawei get a strategic head start.

Over the past two years, Huawei has been striving to create a relaxed, free environment that enables PhDs and other top talent to unleash their full potential. They attract like-minded partners, and work together to make a difference and maintain Huawei's leadership in the world.

The PhD Corps working on 5G MIMO is just one prime example of this. Every talented individual has their own domain of expertise. Their potential can be fully unleashed only when they are put in the right positions. To transform their creative ideas into real technologies, trust and guidance from managers is critical. The failure rate related to technical breakthroughs is high, and it is very likely that no breakthroughs will be made at some point in the near future. Therefore, a more scientific performance appraisal mechanism is required.

"Huawei offers us a large platform with plenty of opportunities," says one PhD Corps member. "Anyone can gain vast knowledge here, regardless of their educational background."

"Whether I succeed or not, I hope that my work is seen and recognized," says another.

"I enjoy working on my team because we keep it simple," adds a third. "When we work closely together, there is no nut too tough for us to crack."

They all say they have had their moments of hesitation and frustration along the way, but whenever they achieve a goal, they feel an overwhelming sense of joy and excitement. In these moments, they see that the late nights, the tears, the detours and the setbacks were not for nothing.

A Mobile Network on a Wooden Pole

By Deng Song

Outside an elementary school in the village of Chum, Ghana, a teacher stood beside a wooden pole, silently watching as the engineers positioned, installed and switched on a new cell tower. "It's connected!" said the commissioning engineer after he had successfully made the first call through the new tower. Hearing this, the teacher quickly took out her phone and logged in to her social media account. She yelled with joy as she saw all her contacts start lighting up, and immediately started sending messages to her friends. The news that the internet had arrived spread like wildfire across the village.

Making phone calls and using the internet may seem rather ordinary for many, but before 2017, it was a rare luxury in rural Ghana. However, Huawei engineers turned this West African nation's dream of connection into reality. Using RuralStar, a mobile base station installed on a wooden pole, they created a digital bridge between the African hinterlands and the rest of the world.

How did RuralStar blossom throughout rural Africa? It all began three years ago.

What could Huawei do for the remote villages?

In 2016, Huawei was awarded a contract by the telecom operator M to build new Long Term Evolution (LTE, commonly known as 4G) networks in nine regions in Ghana. As this work was going on, M suddenly came to us with a new request. They asked us to help improve network coverage across Ghana's remote regions. The country had a population of 28.21 million, 5.4 million of whom were unconnected. The majority of these unconnected individuals lived in remote rural villages. The customer urgently wanted us to improve network coverage to gain a larger user base and grow its revenue from voice, data and mobile payment services. This would also help our customer M build differentiated network competitiveness.

However, building base stations across remote areas is expensive. There aren't many people, and the average revenue per user (ARPU) is low. Therefore, it can take a telecom operator almost a decade just to recoup their investment in building the network. The customer asked Huawei to find a way to reduce the cost of building base stations in rural areas. Huawei's Ghana Office developed nearly 10 network plans and dozens of different business proposals, but the customer didn't accept any of them. I remember that in one meeting, after discussing our proposal, the operator's CTO said to me, with some disappointment, "I have grown with Huawei, you know. I started as an engineer, and now I'm the CTO. For nearly a decade, we have been very happy working with Huawei. Is there really nothing you can do this time?"

In October 2016, Deng Taihua, President of Huawei's Wireless Network Product Line, had a semi-annual executive alignment meeting with Li Peng, President of Huawei Southern Africa. "Twenty percent of people in Southern Africa are still not connected," Li said. "Is there anything we can do?"

The response from the wireless team was unexpected. It turned out that they had just set up an interdisciplinary innovation working group whose aim was to restructure the total cost of operation (TCO) for base stations. It had set itself the goal of going deeper, broader and denser with Huawei's wireless networks. The goal of going broader specifically referred to improving network access for more geographic areas and for more people. Data from the Global System for Mobile Communications Association (GSMA) and Huawei showed that 20% of people around the world had no access to wireless networks, 1.3 billion households had no broadband connection, and four billion people were unable to use any form of wireless data services. There was a massive, untapped market for low-cost and wide-area network coverage, and, in particular, a demand in every country for universal coverage. So, since both the region and the product line had the same objective, why not act immediately? They jumped right into the possible next steps at the meeting.

Ghana Office CEO Liu Kang spoke first. He suggested that rural Ghana be used as the location for a pilot, and gave a detailed rundown of what our customer M was looking for in their rural networks. He also described what the Ghana Office had already tried, and the difficulties we were having.

Both Huawei Southern Africa and the Wireless Network Product Line agreed that Ghana would be a good location to try something new, so they moved quickly to launch the next phase.

Two Huawei Fellows,[1] Lyu Jinsong and Pu Tao, led the effort. The product line brought together experts on 2G/3G/4G, sites, antenna feeders, power supplies and transmission. Together, they combined the technical expertise that Huawei had developed over the years in pursuit of universal network coverage. Working across departmental boundaries, they quickly came up with a number of innovative ideas for enhancing coverage.

For example, they suggested taller towers for a larger coverage reach. If we could triple the reach of a single tower, then the area the tower served would increase 10-fold. Even if the tower cost twice as much, we would still be reducing the total cost by a factor of five. However, it turned out that the tower would have to be over 100 metres tall to achieve that, which would make the cost unfeasible.

Tethered balloons? Balloons floating at 500–800 metres above the ground could stretch for dozens of kilometres in all directions, enabling the network to cover up to 10,000 square kilometres of land. However, balloons were expensive because they had to be able to withstand high winds. They were also difficult to operate and maintain, and there were serious safety issues associated with them. This meant that balloons were not a viable commercial solution.

Could we use phones to enhance coverage? If we added an extra shell to the back of our phones, we could boost the power of signal reception. But, this solution would be too complex to implement.

The more options the working group came up with, the more confused everyone became. What exactly were we going to do?

In the end, Deng said that the working group needed to go on a field trip to assess the feasibility of each idea. "Let's visit the villages in Ghana," he said. "We have to survey the sites to really understand what the customer needs. Then we can work out the right specifications for those sites, which will tell us exactly what kind of innovation we need."

Why 'RuralStar?'

In early November 2016, Liu Jun, Leader of the Super Product Development Team (SPDT), specializing in wireless sites, brought three R&D experts to Ghana. The Ghana Office arranged for three cars with drivers and guides. At dawn on the day after their arrival, we all set out into deep rural Africa.

Talking to local residents

The cars rolled out into the villages, with dust billowing around them. The roads got bumpier as we went further from the city, and the grass was higher than the tops of our SUVs. Our phones had reception only intermittently. We knew we were in the Ghanaian hinterlands. Over the next two days, we travelled nearly 1,000 kilometres. We surveyed 10 sites, including radio and TV towers, wireless base stations and satellite relay stations. We also walked into the villages to talk to local residents. This gave us a clear idea of just how hard it would be to set up base stations in these remote areas.

On our way to a site survey, we spotted two young men on motorbikes, waving their phones high in the air to try to find a signal. They told us that they had to drive several kilometres along steep roads just to get a signal and make a call. But it was interesting to find that almost every home had a 2G or 3G phone. It made us realize just how strong the desire and demand for communications was in rural Africa. Bringing digital to every person, home and organization is Huawei's vision – and it is exactly what we had to do for the local residents.

When our surveys were finished, we returned to the office, and everyone began discussing and analysing what they had seen and the best possible solutions.

The key elements of a rural network are transmission, towers and power supply. Fifty percent of Ghanaian villages had no power supply at all, and diesel generators were too expensive, so we quickly agreed upon the use of solar for power supply.

Still, there were several different camps when it came to the question of transmission.

"We have few resources for network transmission. There's almost no microwave network. If we build one, it has to be within the line of sight, but with all the trees around the villages, that's unrealistic."

Locals travelling on their motorbikes to find a signal

"It's often five kilometres or more from one village to the next, and the most remote villages can be nearly 20 kilometres from towns. That's too far to build continuous cell towers. Expanding the coverage of towers would be too expensive, and building towers would take a long time. It would be a month or two before they could even come online. This is not going to be fast enough for the customer."

"If we use optical fibre or satellite, the cost will be too high. It's not realistic."

Microwave, optical fibre, satellite, cell towers – if none of these would work, then what? There was a moment of silence.

"Could we use wireless backhaul?" After a long time, someone finally made this suggestion. The customer had bought LTE spectrum, providing bandwidth of tens of megabits per second. But in rural areas, most of this spectrum was idle. It offered enough backhaul bandwidth to serve the needs of base stations in rural areas. And in the villages, we would not need to build towers; we could simply use poles.

This was a completely new idea, and the meeting once again came back to life. However, concerns arose immediately after the idea was proposed: "We do have a wireless backhaul product called Relay Remote Node (RRN), but it's not ready for use. Its transmission performance doesn't meet the requirements of a base station. The RRN's built-in, low-frequency antennas only have 2 dBi of gain, so it will only work over short distances."

"We could boost the transmit power on the 4G base stations, and replace the chip in the RRN with a more powerful processor. That would increase the transmission distance."

"But the transmission distance will still be inadequate for 4G base stations that are 20 kilometres away."

No one was sure enough, so we decided to report the idea to the product line to decide. Their decision was to try the wireless backhaul plan. It would be more complex for us, but would give the customer a simpler experience. However, the plan would have to be modified to keep costs down and extend the transmission distance.

With that, we put forward what we call a '3-3-3' approach to developing the solution for rural networks using wireless backhaul. The first '3' represents the factors that went into our decision to develop coverage, cost and revenue models in a particular area: population, power supply and transmission. The second '3' refers to three substitutions: wireless backhaul for microwave, poles for towers and solar for diesel generators. The third '3' stands for a three-year payback period.

We chose a rather lovely name for this new solution: RuralStar. We all had high hopes for RuralStar, believing that this new solution could light up rural Africa, connect the unconnected places and give more rural residents quick access to the outside world.

After a survey at a local shop, the visitors posing for a photo with the head of the village

Innovation is constantly happening, making the world brighter for the people who need it most.

Clearing away the obstacles

Wireless backhaul means using the 2G/3G base stations that serve remote villages to transmit data back to the 4G base stations in urban areas, where the data enters the core network. Imagine a delivery system that is not limited by space or geography. Each package (data) is sent over radio wave to the warehouse (4G base station) and then to its target user. Of course, the same also works in reverse.

Over a six-month period, R&D experts on chips, radio frequency (RF) and sites worked closely with the frontline team in Ghana. Together, we verified the feasibility of backhaul solutions based on real-world site deployment scenarios in Ghana. We did not want to change the standard settings of 4G base stations, so we pondered what else we could do to transmit data further while maintaining low costs.

Ultimately, our SPDT Leader, Liu Jun, remembered that more than 10 years earlier, when they were rolling out 450M network connections for a Chinese telecom operator in rural China, they'd used Yagi-Uda antennas, which were very common in rural areas. This would be a low-cost option that could increase gains by a dozen dBi. As the gain would be higher and the directionality would be more precise, the transmission distance could be greatly extended. When Yagi-Uda antennas were attached to our RRNs, tests showed that we could now transmit data as far as 20 kilometres.

The problem was solved!

Of course, the next problem was close on its heels. Where in the village should our poles installed with RRNs be located?

Now it was the turn of the network planning and optimization team to show their skills. However, when we first took them out to one of the villages with their wireless network planning tools, they found that their tools were designed for continuous network planning in cities and suburban areas. They didn't work in a rural setting. Without the tools, we couldn't tell whether we were putting our base stations in the right locations.

So, we used a simple probe solution, which was just a Yagi-Uda antenna attached to a wireless fixed telephone. One person held up the antenna, and attached the antenna to a wireless fixed telephone to measure the strength of the 2G signal it was receiving from the far-off base station. Whenever we connected a wireless fixed telephone, the people from the village would start queuing up to use it. When the villagers got through to their families and friends living in the cities, the reaction was always astonishment. They could hardly believe that their little village now had phone services.

Locals loved using the phone, but expert Guo's arm
was left more than a little tired

The verification worked, but we were still a long way from getting base stations up and running. In many parts of Africa, there were no contractors that were able to provide the iron poles we needed. If we were to manufacture the iron poles in China and ship them out, it would take at least three months. This was an unacceptable delay for our customer. Amazingly, we found that the answer had been staring us in the face all along. In Ghana, power cables were carried on wooden utility poles, which inspired us. These poles were easy to make, would reduce transportation, civil work and labour costs, and would dramatically shorten the build-out time.

But was a wooden pole strong enough to hold up 20 kilograms of base station equipment? Our expert Guo Yaokui and I worked with a few colleagues to measure the height and width of the poles, as well as their composition. We sent the data back to R&D for analysis and verification, and we were told that these poles should be strong enough. So, we told the customer about our plan. They were incredibly excited, verified our proposal again and gave us the green light to go ahead.

There was still the problem of power, and we asked the customer to help us with this. They were very supportive, and offered us a power supply cabinet from their warehouse, which solved the immediate problem. We also started shipping solar panels from China, which we would need to support the RuralStar trial.

The trial was a turnkey project, meaning we had to complete many procedures, such as gaining approval for the land and power supplies, and getting aviation permits and government licenses. This process would take about six months, with support from our operator customer and other partners. Because Huawei had been operating in the country for many years, and had greatly contributed to Ghana's networks, we were able to get some exemptions that allowed us to conduct our trials first and get the permits before the official commercial deployment.

In less than three weeks, we had cleared away all the obstacles in our path. All we had to do now was switch the equipment on!

Installing a base station on a wooden pole took just two days

The best building in a village was generally the school, so we placed our first RuralStar trial base station next to an elementary school in a village that was about 80 kilometres from the capital, Accra. This was a fairly densely populated area, and placing the base station there would help provide network services to over 1,000 people within a 2-kilometre radius.

The customer visited the first base station mounted on a wooden pole

The whole process took just two days, during which time we arrived, started digging, installed the wooden pole, bolted on the equipment, commissioned it and made the first phone call.

When the engineer completed commissioning the base station and made the first phone call, the local residents were overjoyed. They realized that they could get a full five bars of signal by just standing at their front gate, and they kept exclaiming, "Amazing! Unbelievable!" Some just couldn't wait to call their friends from far away, and you could hear them yelling into the phone: "We have a mobile signal here in the village!"

While we were there, one of the Huawei engineers who had not topped up his phone ran out of credit on the very evening the network was finally switched on. There was no store nearby where he could top up. However, the head of the village was able to quickly go online and use his own phone to top up the engineer's account with 50 cedi (the Ghanaian currency). Everyone immediately saw how useful RuralStar could be!

The first trial site operated for two months without any problems, and the traffic steadily increased. Our customer analysed the business results, and found that we had reduced costs by 70%, while the site generated the same amount of revenue as traditional sites. This meant the customer could recoup their investment within just two years. This kind of return on investment was better than anyone had dared to hope for. We set up further trial sites in another three villages, and all of them produced excellent returns.

Our customer finally gave us a big thumbs up. They immediately sat down with us to plan a nationwide rollout. We found that 90% of the country's unconnected villages were suitable candidates for RuralStar.

RuralStar goes global and innovation never stops

A single spark can start a bushfire. RuralStar was a unique Huawei solution, and no other vendor was offering anything like it. Customers and industry organizations alike loved it. Today, there are 500 RuralStar sites in Ghana, and over 110 telecom operators in 50 countries worldwide use RuralStar to serve nearly 40 million people in rural areas. RuralStar has spread from Ghana to all of Southern Africa, Latin America, Southeast Asia, China, and the list goes on.

In Kenya, RuralStar is helping village teachers get hold of educational materials whenever they need them. In Thailand, RuralStar allows children in remote mountain towns to watch videos on their phones. In China, people in the Daliang Mountains, in the southern part of Sichuan Province, can now go online thanks to RuralStar.

At the Mobile World Congress (MWC) 2018 in Barcelona, RuralStar was given the Best Mobile Innovation for Emerging Markets award. The judges said, "Low power with a choice of sources, low TCO, easy to install with minimal site preparation, new battery technology and security features, this ticks all the emerging markets benefits boxes."

Awards ceremony at MWC 2018

I feel extraordinarily proud to have been part of this whole process, to have watched the birth of RuralStar and its enormous success around the world, and to have seen villagers who were overjoyed at finally being connected to the outside world. From start to finish, this journey was a perfect example of how Huawei can turn any challenge into an opportunity. I believe that RuralStar is just the start of Huawei's efforts to connect the unconnected. Innovation is constantly happening, making the world brighter for the people who need it most.

1   Fellow is the highest honour for technical professionals at Huawei. This title is presented to employees who have made creative achievements in and significant contributions to products, technologies, engineering and other domains, and have sufficient influence in the industry.

Continuously Transforming to Make the Best Software

By Liu Wenjie

At Huawei's Golden Code Award ceremony, held at the end of 2018, I found myself inundated by memories as I watched three members of our team walk onstage and receive the award, Huawei's highest honour for coders, accompanied by thunderous applause.

Two years ago, Huawei started developing 5G microwave and other new products, and this almost doubled our workload. Despite the huge pressure we were under, we still decided to rewrite our legacy code to improve development efficiency and quality. Eventually, by adopting completely new concepts and architecture, we optimized the 2.79 million lines of code that we had accumulated over the past 10 years and simplified them down to just 900,000 lines.

This process was incredibly difficult, and could be compared to trying to change the tyres on a car while it was moving at high speed. We encountered many difficulties and there were times when we felt we were not getting recognition for our work. Nonetheless, we ultimately delivered secure and trustworthy products to our customers, on time, and our code surpassed the requirements set by the Huawei Cyber Security Evaluation Centre (HCSEC) in the UK in multiple metrics. In addition, a number of our team's coders really stood out. Therefore, I am convinced that all of our efforts were worth it.

Refactoring our architecture under pressure

Our department works on software platform development for transmission networks. This is similar to developing operating systems for mobile phones, except that we develop software to be used in network communications products, such as wavelength division multiplexing (WDM) and microwave products. The software we develop enables users to enjoy a variety of functions on their smartphones.

As a platform development department, we develop software for more than 10 different transmission products, so we are constantly under huge delivery pressure. In 2016, the Transmission Network Product Line began developing six or seven new products around the same time, including 5G microwave products. The aim was to get all of these products ready for testing and commercial deployment within just a year or two. For such a short time period, our workload almost doubled. Therefore, if we attempted to continue working based on our traditional efficiency baselines, we would be constantly exhausted.

In fact, we had put a lot of effort into improving efficiency by optimizing organizational operations and developing engineering capabilities. The results were good, but we felt as though we were encountering a bottleneck, and the reason was simple. The root cause of the problem was our traditional software architecture. This architecture was the base and framework upon which we developed software, but it had been in use for over 10 years. Because of changes in the environment and the introduction of new technologies and features, the architecture had inevitably become outdated. It was like a mobile phone that had started to become slow and unresponsive. Small repairs wouldn't fix this problem; only thorough refactoring would do.

The concentrated development of 5G microwave products left us with no choice but to resolve the problem of development efficiency. In mid-2016, managers of the Transmission Network Product Line brought in an expert from a Huawei research centre outside China, and asked us to work with him to explore how to improve the architecture. I took charge of this task as our team's new line manager. After in-depth discussions with the expert, I found that his abstract business modelling concepts could completely resolve our problem of software reuse across different products and chips.

The differences between his architecture and our traditional architecture were analogous to the differences between movable type and woodblock printing. In the past, we had to build a new software model for every new chip we supported. But the expert could help us build a unified and general-purpose model that could be flexibly assembled. This would greatly improve the decoupling and reuse capabilities of the hardware and software. With this architecture, we would be able to develop one model and use it for multiple chips, eliminating the need to develop a new model for every single new chip. This would hugely improve our work efficiency.

We set up a technical project team and spent several months carefully assessing the viability of this solution. We finally confirmed that the abstract model could fit into our actual business, meaning that the solution was feasible. But the challenge ahead was enormous, as we needed to rewrite nearly 3 million lines of code using this new architecture. Our team was made up of a little over 80 people. It was almost impossible for us to complete regular product development tasks and additional architecture refactoring tasks at the same time.

"It's too risky," some people said. "If we can't deliver 5G microwave products on time, there will be huge repercussions."

"Although the legacy architecture is inefficient and has many problems, it can still be used to develop the new products."

"Everybody is criticizing the legacy architecture. Can we develop a new piece of software that would be free from criticism for the next six to eight years?"

After many rounds of discussions, we reached a consensus. In R&D work, we should pay more attention to long-term interests, and never stop pursuing a better future, despite the risks we face. But risks cannot be ignored, either. Therefore, we developed a detailed plan and established a small elite team of excellent coders. They included three software experts from the product line, and five or six outstanding employees from our own department. This team aimed to transform our legacy architecture, regardless of the difficulties that might emerge.

Writing the best code possible

Architecture refactoring can be compared to rebuilding an old house, with each line of code serving as a brick. Without high-quality code, even good architecture will only produce poor results. So, before rewriting almost three million lines of code, we discussed what excellent code should look like.

Writing code is like creating a piece of art, so it's hard to form a set of unified standards for defining good code. We finally all agreed that we must write "exciting" code, a word that was often said by our chief software engineer Shen Lihua. But what exactly is exciting code? Looking back now, exciting code is clean code. This means that the code is simple, easy to read, easy to reuse, easy to expand, easy to test and highly reliable. In addition, we also agreed that clean code should have short and simple functions, small code files, little depth of nesting functions and no mesh dependency for files.

To write such code, we first had to choose a coding language. C++ had been used at Huawei for over 10 years. We all knew how complicated it was, and hated the memory management problem that often appeared with code created with the language. So, several technical experts studied and practised using C++11 in their spare time. They found that it had many distinct advantages in terms of coding efficiency and security, and it had also been widely recognized by the industry.

However, we had never used C++11 during Huawei's product development, and we had no support tools for the language. Some people argued that we should not switch the coding language until the appropriate support tools were ready. It would be too risky, they suggested, and too difficult to adopt a new language when we had neither experience nor support tools. But in the end, we all agreed that if we wanted a thorough transformation, we would have to endure inevitable difficulties. So, we decided to switch to C++11 and develop the support tools through practice.

In order to truly implement our architecture constraints and write clean code, we set a lot of minimum standards for the code. This prevented unqualified code from being adopted in our architecture. We referred to the requirements of leading open-source code libraries, and developed strict standards (such as limiting the maximum cyclomatic complexity of a function to five, and limiting function code to 30 lines). Any code that failed to meet these standards could not enter the library. This greatly impacted our coding habits. Since all code had to pass white box testing,[1] the coding workload doubled. The number of lines of code that could not enter the library exceeded 10,000 at one point. More and more people in the team started calling for us to 'recognize reality and avoid idealism.'

We had many heated debates. Although most people felt the transformation was proving to be a painful process, they also acknowledged that good code would improve quality and efficiency. Therefore, we carefully analysed all the activities, from coding to entering the library, and resolved every issue that arose. For example, since we couldn't use the support tool PC-Lint, we used the open-source tool Clang-Tidy as an alternative. Because the coding language and architecture were difficult to learn, we invited experts to teach us. Considering how strict the minimum standards for the code were, we improved the efficiency of implementing these standards, deployed check items locally, and enabled multi-time implementation of the standards during the same period of time. Through these practices, we gradually changed our coding habits.

In our pursuit of excellence, our team members often reviewed and compared each other's code. We rejected all code that was not clean enough. For example, after a key employee from our department excitedly joined our refactoring project, he was very confident when he submitted code for the first time, as he was widely recognized as an outstanding coder. However, his reviewer rejected his code, telling him that it was not clean enough in design, and that he needed to consider the scalability in asynchronous scenarios. He then repeatedly revised and resubmitted code, which was rejected eight times in total. He was unconvinced in the beginning, but after discussions and careful analyses, he found that the design could indeed be optimized. Finally, he used just 200 lines of code for a function that had previously needed 500.

Our team kept moving forward no matter how many times the code was rejected, and never stopped until we produced truly exciting code. If we thought a line of code could possibly be better, we just continued optimizing its design until it became impeccable. New technologies, better code and the thrill of high-level exchanges between experts helped us enjoy coding again.

During this process, a group of software experts enthusiastically put their hearts and souls into the pursuit of perfection, as if they were young students with great aspirations for the future.

Choosing between schedule and quality

The technical problems had been resolved, but we faced greater pressure that came from the outside. Optimizing software architecture during the delivery process could be compared to changing a plane's engine while it was in the air. This inevitably affected our development speed. In addition, the benefits of the optimized architecture were not obvious to begin with, and would take two or three years to really shine. These factors, coupled with understaffing, made people feel as though we were developing software more slowly than before. As a result, many doubts and questions were levelled at us.

We received several complaints from the product line due to delays in the development process. They constantly sent us warning emails, and reported risks associated with our work during meetings at all levels. The product department and our team both came under tremendous pressure.

Our most difficult period came at the end of 2017, when the 5G microwave products entered the pre-commercial deployment stage, and there were only three months to go before a major telecom operator would start testing. At that time, there were still tens of thousands of lines of code that needed to be written. The product line judged that there was a huge risk that we would fail to complete the task on time, so they filed many complaints. In the past, when dealing with tasks that had a tight schedule, the most convenient method was to copy and slightly modify some code, and then submit it. Although this method could cause many problems at later stages, it would at least avoid large-scale delays in delivery.

However, our architecture had been completely refactored by then, with higher baselines for both requirements and standards. That was why we were behind schedule. We then had to decide if we should insist on writing the best code, or lower our standards to speed up the process and meet the tight delivery schedule.

There were two different camps within the team, and we discussed the problem we were facing almost every two weeks, as if we were decorating a house. Regarding how far we should go, the conservatives thought we only needed to ensure that the 'living room' was decorated in a refined manner, and simple decoration would be enough for the other rooms. They reasoned that in this way, we could quickly meet the delivery schedule and reduce the pressure on us from the product line. However, the radicals insisted on maintaining high standards and using the best solutions, materials and engineering to 'decorate every room.'

From my point of view, we needed to adhere to the goal we had set at the very beginning: writing the best code. Poor-quality materials could be used for decoration, but they had a short life cycle and were prone to many problems after some time, such as water leaks, electrical faults and peeling wallpaper. Firmly in the radical camp myself, I believed that we should just stay the course and complete this arduous development process in order to avoid long-term problems.

In the face of the external pressure, we were not alone. The director of the product department, Wang Chuntian, and the process owner, Yang Xi, put huge effort into ensuring that we had a more relaxed external environment. They also gained the support of the product line's management, constantly working to reduce the pressure on us. Meanwhile, we booked a number of meeting rooms to conduct closed-door development. We all left our mobile phones outside, and worked with incredible commitment. At that time, it was quite normal for us not to go home for an entire week. If we felt tired, we would simply make a bed on the floor and sleep in the office.

By adhering to the Quality First strategy, we compensated for delays in the schedule with the delivery of high-quality code. In the past, when we were using the legacy architecture, we could finish coding in as little as two months. However, we always had to resolve many problems later, and that could take another month and a half. Besides, adding new functions later would take a lot of effort. However, with the new architecture, although it took us two and a half months to write the code, there would be fewer problems at later stages. This meant it would only take us half a month to solve them. It was also easier to add new functions at a later date.

After a period of intense development, we delivered tens of thousands of lines of code on time, all of which were of superior quality, to be tested by the major operator customer.

A quantum leap driven by incremental improvements

As we were working day and night to meet our deadlines, a critical design problem was discovered in a chip during internal tests. This meant the chip might need engineering changes, which would cost millions of US dollars. The product line believed this was caused by negligence during early verification of the chip. I received a letter of reprimand for that, and the entire team was overshadowed by the frustrations of not being trusted. We were under huge pressure, but had no one to talk to.

However, even when almost everyone thought that the only solution was engineering change, we refused to give up. Several experts worked for an entire week to find a solution that could solve the chip's problem using software. They worked for another week to write code and perform verifications. And then, finally, at three o'clock one morning, all the verification items were passed. We all yelled, cheered and cried with joy. We were so excited, not only because we had saved millions of dollars, but also because we had used our wisdom to solve what had appeared to be an unsolvable problem.

This critical problem was just one of many that we encountered over the past two years. We had to continually deal with similar challenges and pressure from all directions. We became frustrated when our staff were unable to effectively use the new architecture and technologies. We felt helpless in the face of constant complaints and doubts coming from the product line, which actually made some of us want to quit.

One day, a key project leader I had worked closely with submitted a resignation letter. That was a huge blow, coming at a moment when I was already exhausted from too much work. He told me that he knew the value of this work, but that it was just too difficult, and that we were not getting any recognition for our work. I helped him calm down and talked with him for a long time. He understood the difficulties the team was facing and how understaffed we were, so he agreed to stay until we got through the difficult period.

I was under huge pressure at that time. My performance results were not good, and I only got a B rating for two consecutive years. Some of my best friends even advised me to get a new job. However, I was determined to finish what I was supposed to do, despite the fact that many people did not understand us and I had no one to talk to. One Friday evening, the department arranged for us to watch a movie. I was very upset at the time, as I had just received a complaint from the product line. The movie was really cheerful, filling the room with laughter. Yet, I couldn't concentrate on watching it. I, a man over 30, just sat there in the darkness, with tears flowing down my cheeks.

I walked out of the theatre halfway through the film, and found that it was drizzling. I stopped a taxi and started heading home, but then I realized that some colleagues must be working overtime in the office, as there were still many problems to be solved. So, I asked the driver to turn around and take me back to the office. Our mission was still not complete, so we had to carry on.

During the middle and later stages of the project, 60% of our department's staff had been involved in the architecture refactoring work. As the project progressed, our abilities also improved. Those incremental improvements finally led to a quantum leap, bringing a miraculous turn of events. We suddenly found that the number of failures to meet the minimum standards for the code, and the number of merge requests rejected by the committers (code submitters), were greatly reduced. And, white box test coverage was increasing. In addition, the defect density during iteration was far lower than in the past, and the code was clean, clear and smooth.

The benefits of the new architecture and new code finally began to emerge. The total number of lines of code on the platform was reduced from 2.97 million to 900,000, and our development efficiency greatly improved. As a result, when we developed a new board based on previous versions, the amount of code that needed to be revised was reduced by half. This meant that a smaller workforce was required to support our business. This allowed us to catch up to the delivery schedule, and our 5G microwave products were successful. Huawei's new 5G microwave and WDM products passed more than 120 customer tests, proving their high quality. To our delight, we even found that our new code surpassed the standards set by the HCSEC across a number of key metrics, including repetition rate and cyclomatic complexity.

Positive momentum toward high-quality code

Over the past two years or so, our group of coders with high aspirations has worked together tirelessly to write high-quality code. We have created positive momentum and reached a consensus. None of us want to lower the bar set by our efficient software architecture and quality code. We all know that what we are doing is worthy of a lifetime of dedication. The project leader who once wanted to quit is also still with us today.

Huawei is now paying an increasing amount of attention to the improvement of software engineering capabilities. The company plans to achieve its goal of developing trustworthy, quality products for our ICT infrastructure business over the next five years. At the beginning of 2019, in an open letter to all Huawei employees titled *Comprehensively Enhancing Software Engineering Capabilities and Practices to Build Trustworthy, Quality Products*, Huawei founder and CEO Ren Zhengfei said, "We will begin with the fundamental quality of our code. Coding quality should be viewed as part of our personal honour and reputation." These words deeply resonate with me.

High-quality code is what we strive for, and we continuously move forward with the ideal of developing the best software. I sincerely hope that every one of us has the courage to do the right thing, and unswervingly carry on to the end, attaining our goals. through excellent, exciting code.

---

1   White box testing refers to a method of software testing where the software's intended function is known. Unlike black box testing, white box testing is intended to find flaws and errors in design and specifications, so it relies on detailed knowledge of the program code itself.

The Magical World of Warehouses

By Ren Tianzhu

Just a few days ago, at a dinner party, a man tapped me on the shoulder and said, "Hey, my friend, I really miss the meatballs and Kung Pao Chicken you cooked for us." His words took my mind back to my experience in Turkey. He was working in Huawei's Turkey Office, where I served as a warehouse administrator for several years. To better collaborate with colleagues on warehouse issues, I often invited them for meals I would cook.

"Back then, our relocation allowances were all spent on food, but I felt it was worthwhile," I said. We both smiled, clinked our glasses and drank to the old days. Those days are long past, but I still feel like they could have been yesterday.

26 issues and 1 recipe

In 2011, after I had worked as an export document reviewer for one year, my manager asked me, "Would you like to go to Turkey and serve as a warehouse administrator? Young people should go out and venture into the world." Since I had a degree in logistics and three years of work experience in this domain before joining Huawei, I did not think it would be difficult to work in warehousing. So, I accepted the job, saying, "I'm happy to assume any position that needs me."

On 8 December 2011, right after arriving at the Turkey Office, I was assigned to take stock at a main warehouse located some 40 kilometres away. The warehouse manager, Mustafa, was excited to show me around. The warehouse was more than 6,000 square metres in size, and its six vertical rows of shelves were all packed. Equipment and auxiliary materials returned from sites were piled up like mountains, and unpacked and packed goods were stored together. Even worse, mops and brooms were being piled up with the goods. It was such a mess! I randomly selected several boxes of goods, and their shipping marks showed that they had been stored in the warehouse for several years.

"Why have these goods been here for so many years?" I was astonished.

"You should ask the project teams," said Mustafa, shrugging with his palms up.

What issues were the project teams facing? Why was the warehouse such an awful mess? What had caused such a low inventory turnover? These questions, which Mustafa could not answer, lingered in my mind and made me anxious.

Starting on the following day, I led over 20 workers of the warehouse provider in taking stock of more than three million pieces of material. After a single day's work, my head was swimming. In order to save time, I decided not to return to my dormitory until we had finished the stocktaking. I put several chairs together and slept in the warehouse every night. It was very cold, and there was only a basic electric heater, so I had to sleep with thick clothes and a thick coat on. At work, whenever I felt sleepy, I went outside, grabbed a handful of snow and threw it on my face to keep a clear head. There were no restaurants nearby, so I had to order pizza and Coke for every meal. As a result, I gained 15 kilograms in a month. Since then, I feel nauseous every time I hear the word 'pizza.'

In late December, we finished taking stock and identified 26 issues. The thought of these issues made me feel uneasy even when eating and sleeping. Why didn't project teams use the materials stored in the warehouse? Why was it that all the materials they needed had to be shipped from the port to the warehouse and then urgently go through the inbound and outbound processes in the warehouse? These issues seemed to be caused by overstocking, poor warehouse management and low operational efficiency. After further analysis, I found that they went far beyond that. There were issues with the entire Lead to Cash (LTC)[1] process, from things like customer demand identification, contract drafting, commercial strategy development, network planning and optimization and site surveys, to things like product configuration, integrated planning, resource preparation, management of changes and error-tolerant design. Warehouse issues were closely related to all these activities.

Faced with so many issues, I was at a complete loss as to what I could do about them. I obviously could not resolve all these issues alone. Looking at the growing piles of stock, I felt as though I had ants in my pants. The company had invested vast amounts of money to buy these materials. Their value was more than I could earn in my entire life. What a waste it would be if these materials could not be used! What could I do to improve the warehouse's inventory turnover?

If I could identify the root causes of each issue and get relevant personnel to pay attention to them, it might be possible to find solutions. After careful consideration, a plan was gradually formed in my mind.

The first step was learning about the LTC process, so that I could identify the root causes of the 26 issues. I learned from account departments, product managers, contract commerce specialists, order specialists, planning specialists and the technical team in the upstream, as well as the project team members and subcontractors in the downstream.

I even downloaded the LTC process flow diagram and managed to figure out all roles and business activities involved in the process. The process diagram would have been as large as a wall if it was printed out, so I had to read through it on my computer, bit by bit. Then I made a spreadsheet with the issues related to customers, suppliers, delivery solutions, technical solutions, supply solutions and procurement solutions, as well as the Customer Centric 3 (CC3).[2] I also listed issues related to coordination between all stakeholders in order to find out areas for improvement.

Second, I talked with colleagues involved in every part of the LTC process so that they were aware of the necessity of alignment and collaboration throughout the process. In order to bring together all relevant colleagues, I would often invite them for meals on weekends, which was where my cooking skills came in handy. There are few Chinese restaurants in Turkey. Therefore, everyone was enthusiastic about coming over to enjoy the dishes I cooked, such as braised fish, stir-fried lamb with scallions and scrambled eggs with garlic chives. After the meal, we would usually talk about the 26 issues we were facing and how each activity in the LTC process could be improved.

Applying the logic of supply solutions, I made a special 'cookbook' that listed the types and quantities of raw materials required for each dish. If anyone wanted me to prepare a dish, they had to go to the grocery store to buy the required raw materials based on the recipe. This method gave everyone a better understanding of warehousing and supply issues.

Take Kung Pao Chicken as an example. Since it only needs 250 grams of chicken breasts, buying a kilogram would be excessive.

The same is true when purchasing equipment, which should be purchased based on demand. Cucumbers are used when cooking Kung Pao Chicken and Moo Shu Pork. However, there is no need to buy one cucumber for each dish, as one is enough for both. This is also the case when purchasing auxiliary materials. Each of our country offices can purchase auxiliary materials collectively, based on the total needs of all projects. This eliminates the need for different project teams to submit purchase requisitions individually, thus reducing waste while increasing a warehouse's inventory turnover rate. These best practices were all gone over during our pleasant get-togethers on the weekends.

However, this was easier said than done. It was difficult to ensure that everyone involved in the LTC process implemented these best practices. I spent a lot of time trying to persuade them to take action, but there were almost no signs of improvements. This left me both exhausted and overwhelmed. To make matters worse, my pregnant wife, who was far away in my hometown of Henan Province, fell ill during this period. Yet, I was unable to take care of her, and I felt very depressed. I still remember how I felt when I was standing on the balcony of my dormitory early one morning. I felt the cold wind blow on my face, which made me feel very sad and sorry for myself. I repeatedly said to myself, "I am just a warehouse administrator, and all I need to do is effectively manage the warehouses in my charge. Why have I gone to the trouble of doing so much that is not part of my job description? What's this for?"

This was the only time I can remember that I doubted my decision to resolve all those issues. Perhaps I was born an optimist and would selectively forget painful experiences. I have always known that I'm not particularly smart. It may be my perseverance that has enabled me to achieve something. Back then, I told myself that I must try my best to proceed with what I had decided to do, because resolving those issues would benefit the company and our customers. Otherwise, I would be unworthy of the company's trust and the salary I was paid.

I continued to follow my plan and learned to let data speak for itself. I also published a series of project-based reports to show the expected improvements from my recommended measures. Ultimately, the Turkey Office adopted my proposals and asked all the teams to pursue my improvement measures. These measures included encouraging customers to choose standard configurations while satisfying their requirements for product functions, and making forecasts based on accurate plans. I recommended we should better understand customers' business plans in order to anticipate the potential changes they might make and develop corresponding plans. I also suggested that we should work with customers to conduct site surveys at the pre-sales stage. Thanks to the joint efforts of all personnel involved in the LTC process in the Turkey Office, the 26 issues were resolved step by step.

Eighteen months later, in June 2014, we saw positive results. While ensuring customer growth, the value of the Turkey Office's inventory was reduced from ¥430 million at the beginning of 2012 to ¥213 million in June 2014. At the same time, the number of warehouses was reduced from four to one, and the total area covered by warehouses was cut from 10,400 square metres to 4,000 square metres. Issues like overstocking, failing during the outbound process and having a slow outbound process were all resolved. There were no words to express my happiness, and this achievement reinforced my belief that even ordinary people can make a big difference when they work together toward a common goal.

Going global: From country warehouse administrator to global warehouse manager

In October 2014, I was fast-tracked for promotion and appointed as the deputy director of the Warehousing Management Department. I was no longer managing the warehouses in a single country, but Huawei's warehouses worldwide.

At the end of 2015, Turkey, Thailand and South Africa saw a surge in demand for network equipment and materials as they ramped up their efforts to roll out 4G networks. This caused numerous logistics issues that we had never seen before. One day, the Turkey Office sent a request to the Logistics Department at our company headquarters, asking to add more than 11,000 square metres of warehouses. That was because all three local telecom operators had started building 4.5G networks at the same time, which would require large quantities of equipment and materials with very short lead times. The head of the Logistics Planning Department was worried about this and assigned me to the Turkey Office to get first-hand information.

Therefore, one year after leaving the country, I returned to Turkey. I went from the airport straight to the warehouse, and along the way Mustafa explained the two major issues they were facing. First, internal demands were not being managed effectively. Each project team was saying that their own project was the most urgent, and they even assigned a representative to the warehouse to intervene with warehouse management. Second, equipment and materials were poorly organized and operation lines were lengthy, leading to inefficient material pick-up. These were the two common issues caused by the spikes in demand. After touring the site for a day, I came up with a solution.

At 1 am the next morning, I returned to the office and delivered a report to the CEO of the Turkey Office. Before I started, he joked, "Hey Tianzhu, I'm not sure you can make real improvements in this warehouse."

I could not accept this presumption and immediately made him a big promise. "It's 1 am in the morning on Wednesday," I said. "I will not sleep tonight and will go to the warehouse immediately to help increase shipments. The warehouse is now able to support the shipments of only 30 sites a day, and I promise that on Friday, this number will increase to at least 300. Please come and check on Friday!"

However, I also made one request: "Please ask all unrelated personnel to leave the warehouse immediately. The prioritization of all demands will be centrally determined by the Project Management Office."

He stood up and said with a smile, "Okay, that's a deal!"

With mixed feelings, I returned to the warehouse. That was around 3 am in the morning, and around 50 workers were still there and buried under their work. I asked them to stop the work at hand and gather around me. I shook hands, hugged and kissed them on the cheek, and then gave each of them a Chinese knot as a gift.

I said loudly, "Hey guys, I'm back! But this time I have been assigned here to help you solve your problems, so I am not feeling good about this. I know you are all very capable, and I believe you can pick yourselves up when you're down. Tonight, we must turn the situation around! We can do it!" Mustafa interpreted for me. Hearing what I said, everyone was very excited, with eyes shining, and they cheered their approval.

In fact, on my way to the warehouse, I had already worked out a plan. The key to solving the issues was how the goods were sorted. I got some inspiration from the way supermarkets stock commodities on racks. Specifically, different types of products are placed in rows, making it convenient for customers to see the choices available to them. In addition, all of the same products are placed vertically in a column on each layer of a rack, making it easy for staff to restock anytime. In our warehouse, we could put the same type of materials in the same slots on the first to seventh layers of each shelf, allowing us to easily pick up all the materials that a site required by walking from one end of a shelf to the other. By positioning materials in this way, workers could pick up and ship materials during the daytime and sort materials at night, greatly improving efficiency.

Therefore, I decided to stop the warehouse's outbound operations for 15 hours, and had all workers focus on one thing: sorting materials. The warehouse did not resume outbound operations until Thursday night. On that Friday, the CEO of the Turkey Office visited the warehouse with his team. When he saw that the warehouse's daily shipments had exceeded 300 sites, he turned and gave me a thumbs up.

Once the Turkey Office's warehousing issues had been resolved, I started supporting the delivery operations of 4G sites in South Africa and Thailand. In one project after another, I came to realize the importance of logistics resource planning. We must develop accurate plans and identify risks in advance, rather than always rushing to address the issues after they have already occurred. I decided to prioritize planning and risk identification during my work over the next two years.

Fully leveraging big data

In March 2016, I led a team of six employees to establish a Logistics Resource Planning Department from scratch. Our first task was to develop a logistics baseline system. With this system, we would say goodbye to reactive responses and arbitrary decision-making during logistics planning. The new system would allow us to calculate accurate data and use plans to help avoid resource insufficiency and waste.

In order to develop logistics baselines and an operations system suitable for each country, we extracted the previous 10 years of data from the Huawei Supply Chain Management (SCM) system and Huawei Transportation Management (HTM) system, and performed multi-dimensional analyses and comparisons.

It was a maddening task, as it required numerous verifications and calculations. Every possibility had to be deduced and simulated based on data. At that time, we didn't know the programming language Python; we had to rely on Excel spreadsheets for data analyses. We did math with tens of thousands of Excel spreadsheets that amounted to over three gigabytes in size, and our computers would often crash. Once, it took us an entire 24 hours just to calculate and compare values. However, this approach was dismissed by another colleague during a casual chat. "Why don't you just build a model using the A-star search algorithm," he asked. "It will only take half an hour to do the math." I was shocked, and this inspired me to learn more. I began reading all sorts of books – including *A Collection of Excel Skills*, *Getting Started with Python*, and *An Introduction to Statistical Analysis* – and tried to learn everything I could about big data analytics.

Finally, we managed to set logistics baselines for each country, focusing on four areas: manpower, finance, resources and operations. The baselines covered everything from the volume of materials each warehouse worker picks up per hour, to the logistics cost spent generating US$10,000 in revenue, and from equipment revenue supported by warehouse facilities per square metre to the timeliness and accuracy of warehousing and logistics operations. We then used these baselines, along with a neural network prediction model, to build a logistics resource-planning model that could make rolling forecasts based on business plans, material-on-site (MOS) plans, and other data. From then on, each country office developed logistics plans based on logistics baselines to mitigate risks and reduce waste. Our company's logistics costs were cut by US$57.4 million in just one year, while operational efficiency increased by 19%.

The work on developing the logistics baseline system paid off. After that, I started a data science team in April 2017. Three PhDs and 10 data analysts joined, and we worked together to solve the logistics issues we faced around the world through big data. As the team's leader, I set a requirement for myself: I may not understand how big data technology works in specific use cases, but I must know about its technical principles and application scenarios, and serve as a bridge between data scientists and business staff.

In just one year, I led the data science team to develop 33 models and tools. You may have heard the 'beer and diapers' story. In the 1990s, when analysing sales data, a supermarket manager found that consumers who bought diapers often also bought beer, but the two commodities did not seem to correlate with each other. So, the supermarket started putting beer next to diapers to promote sales, which was a huge success. The supermarket manager's analysis approach later became known as the Market Basket Analysis algorithm.

When we optimized how materials were arranged within Huawei's regional warehouses, we used this algorithm to analyse the correlation between different types of materials. For example, if two types of materials were always shipped together, we could place them in the same location or even pack them in the same box. In addition, we developed an automatic transport route optimization model and an automatic Harmonized System classification tool based on the logistics scenarios of each country. Many tools my team developed have become part of Huawei's smart logistics solution and are used by the company's supply chain teams worldwide.

A 40-day goal in the Philippines

We can get more hands-on experience working in frontline teams than at headquarters. Therefore, after working at headquarters for three years, I wanted to move back to the front lines. In April 2018, I told my manager that I wanted to be assigned to work outside China. I was put in charge of supply chain operations in the Philippines.

The Philippines is an archipelago comprised of more than 7,000 islands, large and small. Bangkas, a type of crude boat, are used to transport passengers and goods between islands. A Bangka is only a little more than a metre in width and cannot take strong winds or waves. In addition, Bangkas are always in short supply, and if we didn't book them in advance, our delivery schedules would be delayed.

A Bangka, the most common way to transport equipment
between islands in the Philippines

The Philippines can be thought of as 'a museum of telecommunication projects,' with 2G, 3G, 4G and 5G projects all co-existing in the country. This leads to complex supply scenarios, which were challenging to our supply chain team.

Just after I had assumed the new position, the CEO of the Philippines Office tasked my department with shortening the time between shipping equipment and materials from a regional supply centre and completing the equipment installation at a site within 40 days. He hoped such an improvement would allow the Philippines Office to make their operations more efficient.

We had to find a way to complete seven activities in just 40 days. These included: international logistics, customs clearance, inbound and outbound processes in the warehouse, local logistics, site installation, and site commissioning and provisioning. At that time, it took us around 110 days to complete all of these activities, and the business volume was still growing at a rate of more than 40%.

It was an incredibly challenging task. However, as a specialized team, our first reaction was not to challenge the feasibility of the CEO's decision, but to discuss how we could achieve that goal. Maybe this is something that is in the DNA of every Huawei employee. As long as a goal is set, we will do everything we can to get there, no matter its difficulty. There will be no turning back. Our only choice is to boldly move forward.

There is no shortcut to success. In order to reduce the timeframe as a whole, every activity must be as efficient as possible. We then developed 13 key improvement measures targeting the relevant activities, based on the Philippines Office's sales and delivery transformation strategies. These measures not only covered our supply chain, but also considered all associated activities. By accelerating logistics and optimizing information flow, these measures would help enhance the company's operational capabilities and create more value for customers.

One example was how we simplified the order model. In the past, a customer order contained many items, and mapping the customer's item codes onto Huawei's item codes was a complex process. The mapping process required numerous conversions and translations, leading to high costs. Therefore, we aligned our item codes with those of our customers in order to reduce the number of items in an order and significantly cut costs, bringing benefits to customers.

Another best practice was in optimizing how we packed materials. In the past, we packed each type of material separately, and workers had to unpack all of these when installing a base station. This was both time-consuming and laborious, and it was easy to make mistakes. Now, we pack materials according to installation scenarios. All materials for a base station are put into a single large box, which enhances the efficiency of warehouses and reduces the chance of errors.

Other improvement measures included establishing a site database through advance surveys to increase the accuracy of a site's equipment configuration, developing accurate MOS plans based on site readiness, and changing the stockpiling model to on-demand shipments for sites. We also reduced customs clearance times and prepared logistics resources in advance when developing MOS plans and sales & operation plans, at national and global levels. With the common goal of completing the seven activities in just 40 days, all departments comprehensively understood and supported the improvement measures.

By the end of 2018, with the joint efforts of all employees of the Philippines Office, 40% of the 6,934 targeted sites had hit the 40-day goal, and the entire process's inventory turnover had been reduced to just 60 days, which was a new record. In addition, the average time for warehousing operations reduced from 4.6 minutes per line to 1.6 minutes per line, down 65%. The goals for large-scale growth, higher efficiency and lower costs were all achieved. But, we did not stop. Instead, we have remained committed to making further improvements.

Over the years, I have always thought of myself as being like a cog in a machine. My role may have changed from managing a warehouse to managing the supply chain of an entire country, but my goal has remained simple and clear: get my job done well and fulfill my job responsibilities. I have always believed that at Huawei, ordinary people can also make a big difference, as long as they have the vision and drive and put in the effort needed to achieve it.

1   Lead to Cash (LTC) is a main business process at Huawei that spans from leads, sales and delivery to payment collection.

2   Customer Centric 3 (CC3) is a project-based cross-functional team, consisting of three roles: Account Responsible (AR), Solution Responsible (SR) and Fulfillment Responsible (FR).

A World of Zeros and Ones

By Bai Sijian

In my second year of university, while most of my fellow students were spending their time fighting monsters and wizards in online games, I built my own game. My first attempt was a racing game, created out of interest and curiosity, simply to see if I could. That first encounter with code showed me the magical possibilities in a world of zeros and ones. At first, I thought that being a software engineer was all about coding. But as time went by, I came to realize that good code is just the beginning. The devil really is in the detail.

A gamer and a coder

My love affair with code began with games. Back when I was in university, most of the boys loved to play online games. In the university dormitory, watching my roommates' fingers flick across the keyboard and over the mouse, and watching the exciting scenes unfolding on the screen, I was filled with curiosity. How could all of this come from software?

I then spent three months trying to code a tiny racing game. This was when I discovered that software is an amazingly creative medium. Those little groups of symbols could become a right turn or left turn. They could become an accelerator or a brake. It was like building a house, from design to planning, and then building, brick by brick. Later, I started looking into 2D and 3D games. My mind went into 'search' mode: class libraries, game engines, coder communities – I explored, joined, participated and competed. Once I'd learned the ropes, I started to play. Creating games just made me enjoy software even more. When it came to our thesis presentation upon graduation, my coding skills lifted my scores into the top 10 of the entire university, and I was overjoyed.

Before joining Huawei, I worked at an international software design and consulting firm for a while. That company had a deep engineering culture: they were always pursuing the most beautiful code, agility, open source, geeky ideals and monetization of ideas, while holding all code to the highest standards. This environment gave me a new understanding of what software could be, and my skills quickly matured. The ideas I learned there have informed my career ever since. At the end of 2016, with nine years of work experience under my belt, I started working at Huawei, in the Xi'an Research Centre.

New framework? If you're ready, we're ready!

Every software developer knows the importance of refactoring. When it becomes just too expensive to maintain the code in a system, it's time to refactor.

When I first arrived at Huawei, it was clear that the work environment was different from where I used to work. At Huawei, everyone was very focused on following the originally defined plan. We must deliver the product! We must hit our milestones! Following the plan was much more important than responding to changes. The question of how to write the best possible code was barely even considered.

For a code fanatic like me, this was ... challenging. My code OCD was constantly triggered. I found that the project I was assigned to work on used very old versions of the architecture and coding language. Because these versions were so old, there was no testing framework, resulting in regular problems with newer functions. As for refactoring, we didn't even know where to start. Every time we changed a single line of code, we had to recompile the whole thing, which took 5 minutes every time. Debugging could not be performed locally, and because the environment code was compiled, debugging could not be performed remotely, either. To make things worse, the debugging environment was shared, so we had to wait in line for our turn. Sometimes verifying a new feature would mean a long, long wait. I thought that if we could fix these problems, then coding, debugging and self-verification could all be completed a lot faster, and we could save a lot of resources in the development environment.

To get the project team on board with my ideas, I decided that I would first need to produce the new code framework. I worked on this in the evenings, after each working day had finished. It took two months, but I finally had what I needed for a showcase, and worked up the courage to reveal it to everyone. Fortunately, everyone was very pleased with my bold experiment. A new project during the following month put it to the test.

The project manager came to me and asked, "Sijian, are you ready to try out your new framework in place of the old React framework?"[1] It was a lovely surprise, but at the same time, it was a huge challenge!

I asked the guys in my team: "Are we up for this?"

"If you're ready," they replied, "then we're ready!" It was inspiring to be trusted like this, and with a team behind me, I felt that my capacity was multiplied!

With that, our new approach was put into action. Of course, nothing ever goes quite according to plan. In the first month after we made the switch, we had to play whack-a-mole with a range of security issues and historical hangovers. Throughout that month, we just put our heads down and kept grinding away at the issues one by one. There were some dissenting voices, but we stayed focused on the job: where there is a problem, fix it! What surprised us was just how quickly the issues were fixed. By the second month after the switchover, the system was basically stable.

After that, everyone in the project team was able to do both coding and debugging on their own desktop cloud. Rather than coding the front end first, and then the back end, as we used to, we could work on both simultaneously. Instead of testing one use case, and then marking it with a version release, we could now get our use cases for free every time we updated a component. This made it possible to have a more complex local testing environment. When we refactored the code, we also decoupled the differential layer and general logic layer of databases, and streamlined the functional code needed to generate dynamic Structured Query Language (SQL) scripts in multi-database scenarios. This process reduced the volume of the code from 96k to 37k lines, which greatly reduced the code defect rate and maintenance costs.

Sometimes a small but bold change can massively boost the speed and quality of our coding.

Forged in the fires of code reviews

One day, during a team code review session, the team leader said to one of our developers, "Zhang, your code represents a God object (a single piece of code used for multiple functions). There are over 1,000 lines. They don't comply with our coding standards! You're going to have to refactor this."

Zhang quickly explained, "I didn't write this; it's old code. And the schedule doesn't allow for this section to be redone. I don't think there's going to be time in this release."

"Someone has to be in charge of every object. If there isn't time, then we have a dedicated refactoring process. You can enter it into the process, and the time to do it will be accounted for in the next release schedule. The ticket goes to you first, and you follow it up. Everyone picks through this and says what sort of code smell they can find," the team leader explained.

Long methods, primitive obsession, divergent changes, pointless comments – the team piled in with a list!

Zhang couldn't put up much of a defense against this stack of evidence, so he just said, "OK, I'll work out how to refactor this, and then I'll get back to all of you."

In the end, we worked out a three-step method for improving the efficiency of our code review. Step 1: Showcase – what have you done? Step 2: Explanation – how is it designed? Step 3: Check the code in snippets, looking for problems in the logic, style or compliance with coding standards.

These three steps were gradually integrated into a process, and our code review sessions were cut from one hour to 30 minutes. With the new system, we found that team members who were usually quite hesitant about speaking up became some of the biggest talkers.

One day, Gu, a young colleague who I was mentoring, called for a code review.

"Gu, the code for this function is really concise! It's nothing like the copy-and-paste stuff you would show us when you first started!"

Gu looked a bit embarrassed. "A customer reported that the code for some of Huawei's functions had become bloated," he said. "Of course we've got to deliver the functions, but I feel that in R&D we should be making sure our code is high quality as well. If we give things a little more consideration, we can write better code."

"Gu, you're not still automatically generating your test cases, are you? There's more to it than just maximizing your coverage!" Everyone chortled at this.

"Of course they're not automatically generated," Gu retorted. "I coded this line by line. We can review the test cases first. I took pages of notes in all those training sessions on testing. Come on, all of you, look at this."

Sometimes, because we were trying to achieve high coverage in our test cases, we would accidentally speed the decay of our testing code.

It was an issue that had vexed us for quite some time. We always seemed to be trapped between high coverage testing and high-quality testing.

At this moment I remembered a conversation I'd had with my supervisor, Li, six months earlier.

Li had asked me, "We've got very high test coverage, so why aren't we reducing the number of issues?"

"Most of our test cases are generated by the system," I answered. "They don't reflect real functions, so the tests are invalid. If we want to change that, then we need to ask everyone to write their own valid tests. We'll have to give everyone training on how to write high-quality tests. And we'll have to give up on our habit of pursuing high-coverage testing."

Li believed I was right. That day, we spoke at length about the situation across several of the project teams, as well as the details of how to phase in better testing. We also touched on costs and how to forestall potential risks. A week later, the process started for all of the teams, and we were on the road to high-validity testing.

These were the kind of situations we regularly encountered during our code review sessions. Within the team, code is collectively owned. When you alter a piece of somebody else's code, you become its new owner. As a result, you gradually developed a sense of ownership and responsibility for the code. We came to an agreement: during a code review session, there are no managers, no rank and no hierarchy. We all just said what we thought. When we disagreed, we argued it out. Over time, our team culture grew into a true engineering culture.

Three tools to shape high-quality code

Within the context of a fierce code review, three topics are heavily rotated in any argument: coding standards, collective review and code smell. These concepts are powerful and appropriate tools for critiquing code.

Coding standards are like the rules of the road that every new driver has to learn before they're allowed in a car. Red lights mean stop, green lights mean go, and if you break the rules, you have to pay fines. There are company-wide coding standards, and our department has drafted its own supplementary coding guide. These are a bit like satellite navigation systems that prevent you from taking the wrong turns once you've decided where you want to go.

Following the same logic, using collective reviews is like appointing everyone as a traffic cop. It doesn't matter what kind of rules you have; you always need people to oversee their enforcement. Collective reviews enable us to oversee how others implement rules and share information. When a driver breaks a rule of the road, they can immediately be informed by other drivers and quickly correct their driving. Anyone who discovers the most offenses and reminds people of them the most often will naturally become the leader of their team's rule enforcement.

Code smell is when a characteristic of code indicates a deeper problem. When food gives off a nasty whiff before going bad, we can take appropriate measures. Code is exactly the same. If code is unstable or has potential problems, it will display indicators of this on the surface. We can induce rewriting or refactoring by identifying bad smells, which stops code from decaying any further.

Once we started using industry best practices and gathered experience through hands-on practice, we quickly improved. Everyone came to realize what high-quality code looks like, what we need to insist on, and what we need to avoid. Through the process, everyone's coding ability is improved, and everyone's knowledge base is continuously refreshed. Gu, who started under my mentorship, is a great example: he is now an excellent front-end web designer who is also recognized by the team as an expert database administrator.

You may have noticed that many software developers are like the masters from kung fu adventure books. They are highly skilled but modest. What they say is brief, but always on point. Their battlefield is a world of zeros and ones, and they ply their trade with a determination never to let a bad line of code slip through their fingers.

I see good code as the result of everyone's voice being heard, even through a fight or argument, and making sure that every problem gets resolved. This does not mean that everything always has to be done the same way. We are not like magazine editors, mechanically reproducing the same impossible standards of beauty. But it does mean that the team reaches internal agreements.

Transformation is a team sport

Trustworthiness is not something that we can simply achieve overnight. And it cannot be won through the brilliance of any individual. Instead, it is the result of concerted efforts. Once our work to achieve trustworthiness begins, the sustained support of the company becomes more important than ever.

To effectively implement the work on achieving trustworthiness, our department began scheduling an extra 10–20% of team time into our projects for refactoring legacy code. As the code architect, I called a meeting every two weeks, where everyone could discuss any problems they had recently encountered, and we would identify some common issues. The chief software engineer would also regularly listen to and collect issues and ideas from team members. These issues or ideas would be discussed, and then most would be fed into the department's work through quarterly reviews.

A few of them would be handed directly to the Geek Squad and followed up. We would break the work down, and the majority of the tasks could each be completed within a week by about three people. Anyone who worked on Geek Squad issues was eligible to win some geek swag. They would be carefully considered for future awards and their work would positively impact performance reviews. Also, to eliminate common issues, we established a set of Common Building Blocks (CBBs) in the department. We ran these on an open-source basis, and the module architect team produced five CBBs, all of which are now used in our code, and working very well.

After ongoing practice and iterations, we managed to upgrade the quality of our code and the skills of each team member. The products that use our code are achieving their stretch goals, and we have received a Quality Gold Award. We put together some of our ideas to achieve trustworthiness, and I worked with a writer from HR to produce a book: *Practical Ideas for Achieving Trustworthiness*. The ideas and case studies in the book were quickly borrowed by many teams, helping them better achieve trustworthiness. We have also been asked by several departments at HQ and in Xi'an to share our experience.

Final thoughts

Young colleagues sometimes ask me, "How can I improve my software skills?"

My message for everyone is that if we are to maximize the potential of every coder, we must provide them with an environment for growth to complement their own personal efforts.

First, trust is the biggest incentive for anyone. The simple phrase, "I believe in you!" is more powerful than any poetic praise. It is the foundation of any strong team. Rather than hedging your team members in, why not let them go out and try? There is no need to fear unknown risks or daunting challenges. As long as your team is committed, then bit by bit, step by step, you'll get there.

Second, every team member is equal, and everyone has the right to be heard. Don't make the team's work a space for asserting technical authority. Excessive reliance on authority does nothing for teams or individuals.

Perhaps you've heard of the flywheel effect. Starting a flywheel takes massive amounts of energy. You have to put work into every turn, and the more work you put in, the faster it turns. When the wheel reaches a certain speed, it has its own internal momentum, which is very powerful indeed.

Habits never change on their own. They always require a push. Currently, Huawei's transformation program for achieving trustworthiness is still at the stage of 'starting the flywheel.' Every push is hard work, and to overcome the resistance and get the wheel turning will take a united effort. But this effort will be recognized, and the work we put in will be rewarded. When we go all out to achieve a goal, we will ultimately see real change.

1 React is a JavaScript library for building user interfaces. It was designed to support the development of large applications in which data is changing continuously.

Midge Tornadoes

By Xu Haiming

The two treasures of Huawei Malawi

The email came from Han Xinli in the Zimbabwe Office when I was receiving training at Huawei's headquarters in Shenzhen in 2007. I was notified that I had been assigned to Malawi. After hours of research online I still had no idea where it was. So before I left Shenzhen I told my parents that I would be working in Zimbabwe. As far as I know, they still think that Malawi is a province in Zimbabwe.

At that point, there was me, and there was Wang Yaofeng, and that was about it for Chinese employees based in the southern African nation. When we arrived, there was no furniture in the new apartments they'd rented for us, not even beds, so we hung up our mosquito nets and slept on the floor. Mr Zhang, the cook, found us some big cardboard boxes that had held fridges or TVs, and laid them out on the floor to stop us from catching cold. After a couple of days, both Wang and I broke out in mysterious red spots all over our bodies and began itching like crazy. It turned out that the boxes had previously served as sleeping mats for dogs, which had had fleas. Mr Zhang has been apologizing to us ever since.

Malawi is named after Lake Malawi, Africa's third largest and deepest freshwater lake. It goes down 706 metres at its deepest point, and covers an area of 29,600 square kilometres. The lake is a boundless paradise of crystal clear water. It is also one of the world's largest breeding grounds for midges – a type of tiny, swarming fly. At dusk in the rainy season, I would sometimes see what looked like tornadoes over the lake – black pillars extending high into the sky. They were not, in fact, tornadoes, but billions of midges ascending from the water. On the subject of flying parasites, we did not know how to protect ourselves properly from mosquitoes early on, and we contracted malaria constantly. One wireless product manager, Zhang Yan, was infected four times in a single month while out on a Telekom Networks Malawi (TNM) phase II project: one dose of malaria each week. Eventually we learned to put up screens and nets, and to get our buildings sprayed every two weeks. We learned better personal mosquito awareness as well, and these days Huawei employees rarely fall victim to the disease.

Midges forming a 'tornado' over Lake Malawi

Of all the stories that the Malawi Office might tell, none is as marvellous as Mamo. In 2006, Mr Zhang bought a puppy from a roadside vendor for US$3, hoping that it would grow into a useful guard dog. From the day Mr Zhang brought it home, Mamo would be the author of his own tale. He began by beating up every male dog within a five-kilometre radius of our office; he went on to pacify the female dogs, of every size and shape. Mamo could also distinguish the sounds of different vehicles. When one of the company cars pulled in, he would pay it no attention whatsoever, but the first time any unknown vehicle pulled up outside, Mamo would position himself right next to its door. Visiting suppliers or customers often didn't dare get out of their vehicles until one of us went out to welcome them. The second time the same car returned, Mamo would return to his usual disinterest.

In the early hours of one November morning in 2010, armed robbers threw poisoned meat into the yard of our compound (our office and living quarters were all together in the same property). We had six dogs, and all of them ate the meat, but when the robbers climbed over the walls, Mamo attacked them just the same. By the time the police arrived, the dog had chased them off and kept us all safe. Mamo is still on guard in the Malawi Office, a greater warrior than Mr Zhang could ever have dared to hope for.

The legendary Mamo

Once we won our first contract for the TNM core network and wireless network, operations in Malawi developed smoothly. From five people in 2007, the office has grown to 50 people, and we record stable equipment revenues in tens of millions of US dollars every year. Before I left, many of our customers told me why they preferred to work with Huawei Malawi. The first reason is that we give customers immediate service, at any time. This is because we have been in the country longer than other vendors, and we have built up a fully localized service network. The second reason is that we help our customers succeed. For example, Malawi had frequent power outages, and afterwards certain vendors' equipment would sometimes not restart. We would always help our customers reboot their networks, Huawei and competitor equipment alike, and our customers ultimately came to appreciate the humility and respect we showed them. Huawei's business is concentrated in two key cities, Lilongwe and Blantyre. One year, my driver and I clocked up over 100,000 kilometres responding to customer calls, making the round trip of over 600 kilometres between the two towns three times every week.

My life changed, and it all started with the pledge we'd made: to deliver or go down trying.

A life changed by a pledge

In mid-2008, I was selected to support a full turnkey project for 300 sites for the South African operator MTN in Zambia. I was the contract manager, responsible for ensuring contract execution and managing any contract adjustments. That project was our first major turnkey delivery project in the region, and the customer's deadline was delivery in 12 months, from a standing start. We had to complete site preparation, foundation, construction, equipment installation and network connection. Since we didn't have enough experience, nor good delivery resources in the area, the project team had not developed a good plan, and their lack of progress was causing worry. The deputy general manager for delivery, Li Yueming, took charge and began chairing daily meetings right after dinner. We met every day for 180 days, going over our progress and solutions every evening. It was a hard, hard slog. This project was my first chance to sample what delivery means, and how it feels to really get down to work.

In May 2008, Zhao Dong, who worked on site design, and I wrote an email to the general manager pledging to make our own contribution by delivering 13 sites in 60 days. If we didn't succeed, we said we'd let them send us home. Our pledge was accepted, and the local office assigned us the city of Kabwe. So, Zhao Dong and I named ourselves local project managers, a driver drove us over to Kabwe in a rickety old car, and we got started.

Every day, we loaded the car with three things: our computers, water and biscuits. The computers were our office, the water and biscuits served as rations for the subcontractors and us. The sites we had to deliver in Kabwe were out in the countryside, and were not connected to the power grid, so we were often pouring concrete under generator-powered lights. The generators were temperamental, and apt to go on strike at inopportune moments. But once you start pouring concrete, you cannot stop, so Zhao Dong and I often had to rush about lining up cars to use their headlamps for lighting. We worked with the subcontractors through the night for three days straight so as not to fall behind schedule. We provided them with water and biscuits and kept them pepped up with a constant stream of encouragement. Through a combination of hard work and bloody-minded perseverance, we completed the 13 sites we had pledged within our 60-day limit.

Kabwe was on the way from the capital to the northern and western regions, so the hotel room I shared with Zhao Dong became something of a staging post for colleagues passing through. Those less troubled by conventional niceties would often just double up with us in our room for the night, and in return we asked for nothing more than a few packs of instant noodles. Talking with our visitors from other regions, we realized that the contract delivery conditions were often being significantly revised onsite, but we had not reflected these changes in our price at all, so when Zhao Dong and I returned to the capital, we put together a portfolio of the types of changes often seen in the process of delivery. We collected documentation for the 300 sites, and conducted negotiations with the customer's CTO. It took dozens of meetings, but in the end we achieved an adjustment to the contract of US$3.91 million. That was the first purchase order (PO) I ever signed for the company.

In early 2009, the local office put me in charge of delivery for Malawi. In that job, each day was a crisis. I grabbed every opportunity I could to learn about the technology underlying our products: frames and time slots, spectrums and signals, network architecture, etc. Every time we carried out a product upgrade or fault maintenance, I would liaise with the customer and manage our maintenance teams, so that over time I developed good relationships and trust with our customers' CTOs and other contacts.

Later on, I worked with the team to codify our experience into explicit rules for project management and product operations. Developing clear procedures helped to make the team more efficient and boost customer satisfaction. Later still, because I was able to work well with customer CTOs, the local office promoted me to account manager, and then to head of regional office, head of enterprise business, country general manager, and, ultimately, head of HR.

My life changed, and it all started with the pledge we'd made: to deliver or go down trying.

Thank you to all those who helped me, put up with me, and supported me through the years.

13

Transmission at the Speed of Light

By Jeffrey Gao

"Lucent is the industry leader. How does the equipment you are making measure up to theirs?"

That was the question that our founder and CEO Ren Zhengfei put to us one evening in 1998, when he dropped in unannounced at our lab. Since then, 18 years have flashed by, and today we have a definitive answer to this question.

Green team, world-class ambitions

1997 was a good year for China. The whole country was celebrating the return of Hong Kong to Chinese sovereignty. It also turned out to be a lucky year for me. In Shenzhen, just across the bay from Hong Kong, I was starting my career at Huawei.

Back then, I was working in the transmission network department, in charge of developing network devices that could handle data rates of up to 2.5 gigabits/second, or 2.5G, using the synchronous digital hierarchy (SDH) protocol. We encountered many, many difficulties, and at one point we ran into a problem that we just could not solve, no matter what we tried. We had no choice but to call a vendor outside of China to ask for more information that we could use. None of us could speak English fluently, but in the end it fell to me to make the phone call. I had to bite the bullet. I rehearsed in my head over and over again what I was going to say, but when I heard the voice on the other end of the line say, "Hello?" my mind went completely blank, and I forgot every line I had prepared. "Please give us a demo board," I stammered. When the call was finally over, my teammates all yelled at me for not saying clearly what issue we were having. But, unexpectedly, the vendor faxed the diagram of the demo board to us the very next day. That diagram helped us work through the issue. That was a very happy moment for me.

The New Times Building, former home of Huawei R&D

Our R&D team, with an average age of under 30

One year after we developed this product, I was sent to a small town in Chongqing to help set up some equipment for our customer there. Unexpectedly, I received a call from one of the company secretaries. She told me to get back to Shenzhen as fast as possible and to start packing for a telecoms expo in Moscow. In the chill of early spring, I flew to the Russian capital.

Huawei was the only exhibitor from China at the event. Later, we won a contract to provide a set of SDH transmission equipment in the Russian city of Bryansk, and that got our whole international development off to a good start.

Next, we started to develop a range of multi-functional products with 10 gigabits/second, or 10G, of bandwidth. At the time, this speed was known as a tough target. Only the world's top companies had the capacity to create products at this level. But because I had worked on the 2.5G products, I was appointed product manager, leading a team of green young men as we took on this world-class challenge.

Looking back, it's obvious that we were 'fools rushing in.' We had no experience developing this type of equipment, and there were no books or papers that we could use as a reference. So, we had to figure it all out ourselves. Every step of the way, we cast around for the right way to go next. We would try a number of different ideas, and test them to see if they worked.

In fact, we had a lot of arguments over what kind of design we should use, and they often got quite heated. On one occasion, the guys in the lab next door thought there was some kind of fight going on, and hurried around to break it up! Sometimes the arguments would get more and more intense without any sign of agreement in sight and, in the end, I had to step in and make a decision: we're going to do this, because I'm the boss.

But despite all the differences of opinion, we were a tight-knit team. When we got off work, we would go to a small restaurant nearby, order a big plate of fried noodles and some shish kebabs, then chat and laugh the evening away. We were always 100% direct with each other, saying exactly what we thought. That way all the different possibilities and attendant risks could be worked out. It was a good way to minimize the chances of making a big mistake.

Before we launched the product, we invited some of China's leading specialists in this technology to come to our manufacturing facility and run some tests. During this period, none of us went home at all. We laid down mats on the floor of our factory in Shenzhen and lived there for two weeks. The last test was to run the equipment continuously for 72 hours in environments ranging from –10° to +55° Celsius. At the end of the 72 hours, all of our little indicator lights were still burning steadily, and we knew that we had finally completed our toughest challenge. I still have fresh memories of that day. I walked out of the plant at 5 o'clock in the morning of 12 May 2002, to find our Shenzhen campus looking more beautiful than ever before. The rays of the early morning sun lit up our scarlet, fan-shaped logo, and it shone like a beacon.

Later, Wei Leping, chief engineer of China Telecom, visited Huawei and spent a good long time looking at our products. He said, "I would never have imagined that a world-class product like this was developed by a gang of young twenty-somethings."

Never forget the core strengths

But one successful product is not enough to keep a whole department growing healthily. We were determined to build up a suite of core strengths, including chip development, technological innovation and collaboration with external partners.

Buying chips from other vendors was pricey. With that kind of high cost base, we found it hard to make products that would deliver real value for money. So, from the very beginning, from our very first generation of transmission products, we had been working on developing our own core chips. Even though we were still very understaffed, we kept some of our best people working on this problem.

At the time, He Tingbo (who is now the president of HiSilicon) was in charge of chip development, while I was responsible for product development. A lot of the same instruments and meters are used to run tests for both products and individual chips, so she and I frequently got in each other's way as we sought out resources. Being a gentleman, I would always allow her to use the instruments first, but over the long term this was not sustainable. And so, we came to a gentleman's agreement: She would have priority access during the day, and in the evening the equipment was all mine.

Our persistence and hard work did pay off in the end. Our first generation of core chips were delivered just as we had hoped, and we went on to develop a series of chips that sold in the tens of millions. All this enabled us to build transmission network equipment that remained competitive and cost-effective over the long term.

One of the core technologies we are very proud of is our algorithm for Automatically Switched Optical Networks (ASONs). In many countries, such as Brazil and India, optical fibre cables used to break frequently because of the difficult terrain, and that would cause the phone and internet signals to cut out. We designed ASON technology to deal with this problem. ASON is like satellite navigation for a network. Imagine that the fibre cables are the roads, and the phone or internet signal is a car. When one road is blocked, ASON will find a new route so that the signal can still get to its destination. When ASON was used in the networks of one Indian telecom operator, its CTO sent us a very satisfied comment. "Ever since we started using the ASON technology," he said, "there have been no communications outages due to broken fibre."

Huawei was also the first vendor in the industry to propose and develop end-to-end subnet management technology. Our technology offered a WYSIWYG (what you see is what you get) interface and smart routing. It made communications network maintenance very simple. By providing both software and hardware, we were able to significantly boost the overall competitiveness of our products.

At about that time, many countries were launching national broadband strategies and urgently needed efficient, flexible ultra-broadband fibre networks. We spotted the opportunity and piled on the pressure in our ultra-broadband R&D. That was how our switching equipment for Optical Transport Networks (OTNs) came into being.

In the communications sector, before launching any new product, vendors must always consider the issue of interoperability with equipment made by other companies. Standards are the most common way in which this problem is solved. Huawei was the first company to make this kind of equipment, so one of the first issues we had to consider was how to update the relevant technical standards.

At the time, we were a very new player. We had almost no influence on any of the standards committees. At the outset, the problem was not so much how to get agreement on our new standard. The problem was that the committee wouldn't even put the issue on its agenda. Soon, we realized that we could not win this battle ourselves. We needed allies.

We sought help from China Mobile and China Telecom. They were already influential voices in the global communications sector, and they were also looking to diversify and expand the industry, so they were natural allies for us. At a meeting of the China Communications Standards Association, we were finally able to drive a thorough discussion of the OTN standard proposed by Huawei. Based on our customers' commercial imperatives, we hammered out how the standards would evolve. Then, we worked with our partners and customers outside China: we delivered lectures and participated in workshops on these standards in global standards organizations. By that time, we had a strong set of arguments and materials to back up our position. We had powerful supporters. And the technology we were proposing was good; it was forward-looking, but backward compatible, and we had taken on board many different suggestions along the way.

Ultimately, we were able to evolve the standards, one step at a time. By the time the standards took shape, our proposals accounted for 75% of the content of the OTN standard. That gave us a strategic edge in the ultra-broadband optical transmission sector. Within three years, we developed the equipment, which supported a big jump in the sales for our fibre transmission products over the next few years.

But building up our core technical strengths was not something we could do entirely on our own. We needed to find help externally. In 2002, a company that specialized in long-haul wave-division multiplexing (WDM) was up for sale. So, we asked Huawei corporate leadership for approval to acquire it. The dotcom bubble had only recently burst, and cash was very tight. Our leadership had all taken pay cuts themselves. But still, they thought the technology was promising, and they approved the acquisition.

This bold and wise decision later came to be regarded as the best deal our transmission networks team ever made, helping us roll out our ultra-long-haul WDM solution in no time. This solution helped us quickly grow into the global market leader in this space – a lead we maintain to this day.

The selection of the right path also played a key role in building the company's core strengths. In 2005, we wanted to launch our own microwave transmission equipment. However, the microwave market was well served by established vendors, and there was no demand in China. It seemed that we would be forced to go head-to-head with experienced rivals in the international market.

At first, we wanted to start selling in the traditional microwave equipment market. However, we were not sure whether we could succeed. Then, during a visit to Vodafone, they told us there were already more than enough companies selling traditional narrow-band microwave transmission equipment. However, they hadn't decided yet which vendor would get the opportunity to meet their next-generation Internet Protocol (IP) microwave needs. These comments added to our determination to go all out to develop and sell microwave transmission equipment for IP networks. Subsequent events would confirm the wisdom of that decision.

Our IP microwave transmission team was bidding for the Vodafone project, but Huawei had no brand recognition in this field. Our frontline sales guys and the boys in R&D worked in close collaboration, 24 hours a day, guiding us through three rounds of tests and technical negotiations before we were able to make Vodafone sit up and take notice of Huawei's IP microwave offerings. We shifted Vodafone's perception of us, and their disbelief and suspicion gave way to gradual recognition of our strengths. In the end, we won the Vodafone contract, and this demonstrated that the Huawei microwave team had what it took to be the partner of a world-class operator. It made Huawei's name in this sector.

But our celebrations were short-lived. Vodafone demanded that we pass their admission tests within seven months. That put our R&D team under a lot of pressure. We were using a whole new set of chips and immature technologies, but we were able to overcome all of the teething problems. Moreover, we made a forward-looking shift in the software architecture. Finally, during

Chinese New Year 2009, when most people were home spending time with their families, the R&D team came together for a final push to get us through the Vodafone admission tests. Our products went on to become a huge success in the market, and other operators across Europe flocked to build a relationship with the Huawei microwave team.

We will conquer 100G!

Now that we had mastery of the core technologies, and we had successfully created 2.5G and 10G products, we were ready to push on to new peaks of 40G and 100G. First, we made a bold push for 40G bandwidth. This placed our equipment in a class above any competitor's, and our 40G solution quickly became the new standard in Europe and other developed markets. Coupled with a new architecture that we launched for OTNs, our WDM products for fibre transmission became the market leader in 2008. Even so, we didn't let up the pressure for one moment. We started focusing our R&D efforts on developing a solution that would operate at 100 gigabits/second (100G).

Unlike our previous products, 100G represented a real leap beyond the existing state of the art. It was a real moonshot. We gathered some of the top minds in fibre technology and drew on many interdisciplinary insights. Successful completion required the combined resources of Huawei and many external partners.

In November 2008, while our 40G product was still in the final stages of development, the Fixed Network Product Line set up a joint team to develop a 100G solution. The team was given the name '2091.' This team of several hundred members was scattered around the world – it was a team on which the sun never set! Led by a core group of PhDs and industry experts, 2091 kept working 24 hours a day on a new dash to victory. In terms of management, we made a lot of innovations for this team. We made sure that each of our expert contributors was given the respect and trust they deserved, so that they could all do the work that they had always dreamed of doing.

June 2011 was a defining moment in the story of our 100G project. Our chips were being fabricated in Japan, but on 11 March 2011 the Fukushima tsunami wreaked havoc on the entire country. As a result, our chips couldn't be shipped until 8 June. But, we were due to start services for our customer in the Netherlands, Royal KPN, on 15 June. Five days after that, the product would be officially launched at the Institute for International Research (IIR) forum. From shipment of chips to customer delivery, we had just seven days. No one thought we could make it.

"Even if we only have a 1% chance," we said, "we still commit 100% to getting it done." The entire 100G team was locked in a race against time, and we put the pedal to the metal. The team developed a plan for fast product commissioning called 'Mt Emei,' and went over and over every detail. We put in place contingencies for every risk. And, we stationed top people at the manufacturing and assembly sites to make sure any problem could be spotted and instantly resolved.

13 June, 6:15 pm: The Mt Emei Task Force boarded a flight from Japan to Hong Kong.

13 June, 10:05 pm: The Task Force arrived in Hong Kong and went immediately to the Huawei Shenzhen R&D facility. With 'Deep Sea,' they would execute the high-speed assembly and commissioning of the 100G solution.

14 June, 0:05 am: 'Deep Sea' and 'Rich Soil' were successfully united.

14 June, 8:12 am: Every top specialist gathered in the opto-electronic lab and started preparation.

In the early hours of 15 June, we split into two groups – one headed for Amsterdam, the other for Luxembourg. However, when we arrived onsite at the customer premises, for some reason, the equipment did not work. We had made a promise to the customer, and they were waiting with a billboard ready to unfurl, and a press release ready to send out. You can imagine how much pressure there was on our shoulders at that moment. We still believed there would be a solution. The team in Shenzhen stayed online with us and gave us ideas on how we could address the issue.

Unfortunately, the equipment had gone on strike, and nothing would conjure it back to life. We refused to give up and kept on eliminating possible causes, one by one. We upgraded the software. The technical sales manager stood off to one side and received a call from the customer at 10 o'clock that night. The customer was starting to worry. Were we actually going to be able to deliver this product or not? But all our hard work had not been in vain. At 11:30 that night, the historic moment finally came when data began to flow through the new system. We all jumped for joy, our eyes brimming with tears of excitement.

As scheduled, on 20 June 2011 Huawei and Royal KPN jointly announced Huawei's 100G solution at the IIR forum. Over 180 customers watched the presentation on how the equipment worked, and saw data flowing in real time from the equipment on the networks of Royal KPN. At the conference, our KPN contact said, "Huawei has many very professional people with many years of experience. I hope that we can continue close collaboration with them in the future. We will invite our customers to observe our 100G tests, because these tests are extremely important to our business."

Orders for the 100G equipment poured in after the launch. In 2014, we made our first major sales in the Japanese and South Korean markets, which have the toughest technical standards in the world. Our business was really taking off.

The 2011 IIR forum in Monaco

We still have the same
goal we always did:
to be a leader.

We never stop

We have a special world map in our office. Every time we sell our equipment for transmission networks to a key account (namely, a major telecom operator), we stick a Huawei logo on the map. To date, we have delivered transmission solutions to over 80 of the world's top 100 operators. These solutions serve more than 3 billion users, tens of millions of businesses, and connect hundreds of millions of households. We are one of the world's most trusted transmission network providers. The rise of our transmission networks has also contributed to the boom in the communications market. In the early years, when only a few companies were able to deliver fibre communications solutions, the cost of rolling out a transmission network was quite high. Our hard work has helped cut the cost of communications so that services are affordable for everyone.

Today, the demand for data is growing explosively, driven by 4K high-definition video and the upcoming 5G mobile networks. And, the convergence of information technology with communications technology means that we have an opportunity to roll out simplified networks that deliver a premium experience. Underpinning all of these new developments is fast data transmission infrastructure, and that is exactly what the transmission networks team delivers. So, for us, the market is huge. Afloat on these vast seas of data, we still have the same goal we always did: to be a leader. But now, we are not content to lead just in terms of sales. Huawei wants to be a leader of the industry in every respect.

We never slow down, never ease off, never stop pushing the limits!

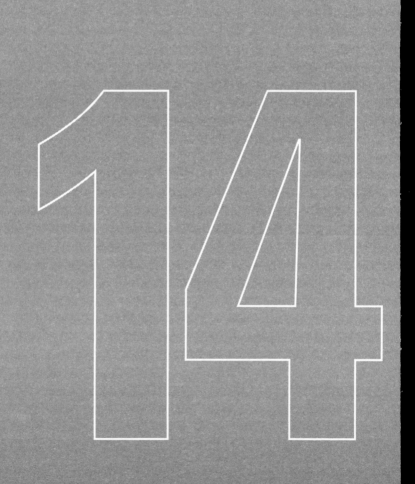

Lightning Chasers

By Xiong Ying

I spent the entire summer of 1998 'putting out fires' with two other colleagues.

That summer there were many thunderstorms, and Huawei's equipment suffered major damage from lightning strikes. First it was the transmission products, followed soon after by an enormous number of switches and access equipment. As there was no dedicated team focused on lightning protection, we were assigned as provisional 'firefighters.' Each day there was a new emergency that left us scrambling to catch up. On one occasion, during an emergency, I found myself rushing back to my room to grab my bags, the driver below desperately honking the car horn. I was in such a hurry to get back downstairs that I slammed right into a glass door. I broke my nose and smashed my glasses to pieces.

Upon arrival at the test site, as I held the burnt board in my hands, I didn't have any tears left to express my despair. I did not have an understanding of the design and standards for lightning protection, so I was working completely blind. I might wriggle my way out of one issue, but would get caught by the next! I felt really bitter about things at the time, and I would mutter to myself, "Why is our lightning protection so outdated?"

Looking back on all of that now, it almost seems comical, but it was real. There are many incredible stories to tell about how we moved from fearing and avoiding lightning to actively pursuing and guiding it.

Best forklift driver among R&D staff

Prior to 1999, because of a lack of design consideration, equipment DC power slots had weak protection against lightning, and were highly susceptible to damaging lightning strikes. As we had some experience, we installed lightning protectors on DC power slots, which helped to temporarily solve the issue. However, to eradicate the root of the problem, we had to form a dedicated team that could incorporate lightning protection into the product design stage. With a broken nose to prove my experience, I also joined that team.

During our first meeting, only a handful of people sat in the expansive room and stared at each other. Could the few of us new recruits really solve the issue of lightning protection in Huawei's major product lines? Luckily, not long after that, several Huawei experts with experience in lightning protection also joined the team, finally enabling us to unite as an effective operating force.

We didn't have much hard data at hand, let alone any online courses. All we could do was use our spare time to read books, study theories and look up case studies. When we didn't understand something, we would seek out one of our supporting experts. If they couldn't address the issue, then we'd do more reading. We even called in one of China's leading experts in lightning protection in the communications industry, Liu Jike, to give us some lectures. He was 'the best of the best,' and could provide authoritative information about lightning protection. We desperately wanted to snatch at every straw, in the hope that one might be the one that could save us. We were thirsty to study any training materials or notes we could get hold of, and treated them all like rare treasures to be pored over and studied endlessly. This was the process we adopted to establish port lightning protection specifications for Huawei equipment.

After receiving training, we eight core team members were each assigned one of eight important products involving wireless, switches and access networks. Each of us began our respective attempts to develop lightning protection circuits, dealing with different types of ports, and trying to match lightning protectors to different circuit designs. To decide whether or not the protectors were up to snuff would require testing. It was then that we realized that the company didn't have any instruments to simulate lightning strikes. So how were we going to test our plans?

Finding the right instrument immediately became our most urgent task. We asked peers in the industry, having heard that the instrument we needed might be in Guangzhou. We were going to have to move a huge equipment cabinet onsite for the testing. Trucks weren't allowed in the city during the day, so we had to wait until the wee hours of the morning to enter Guangzhou from Shenzhen with our vehicle. If you were there, you would have seen a group of old fellas in the middle of the night, lugging a huge cabinet weighing hundreds of kilos onto a truck along with soldering irons, cables and a pile of other tools, and heading into the city. After we arrived at our destination, because the cabinet was too heavy, we still had to use a forklift to get it down and into the lab. We had to go through this process regularly over a period of several months. I quickly became an expert forklift driver, and was known as such by my colleagues.

'Workaholics' on the production line

As soon as we started working in the lab, we implemented the plans we had pulled together through experience. However, the first test revealed problems: the circuit plans we had prepared did not provide effective protection for the communications ports. This result was to be expected, since the informational materials we had referenced had not been written for communications equipment. There were sure to be differences, and we had to carry out the tests while also looking for the right circuits for the company's products.

With the circuit plan validation, for example, based on our original estimations, we only installed a lightning protector on the lightning protection circuit. However, it was found to be inadequate right from the start of testing. Luckily, we came prepared, added another protector and confidently went back to test again – only to be faced with failure once more. What was going on? I was getting worried by this point. If we couldn't figure it out onsite, we'd have to head back to Shenzhen to make further preparations, which would mean the entire week had been wasted. I was adamant that we find a solution.

I was the one who had installed the lightning protection circuits, so I looked at them carefully again and realized an inductor – the component used in conjunction with the lightning protector to improve its performance – was missing. So, in a jiffy I opened up my tools and removed the thick copper wire from within the cabling. I then built an impromptu inductor right then and there, which significantly improved the lightning protection performance.

This approach actually worked. I was pretty excited, but the inductor was flimsy and would wobble around if the board was moved. It was a good interim solution, at least, until we could improve upon it in formal delivery production.

Speaking of delivery production, that is another story of sweat and tears. Because a lot of equipment did not give consideration to lightning protection, boards did not provide space for such functionality. We thus had to install lightning protection circuitry into a box, assembling this into a lightning protector. We issued an instruction manual to help technical service engineers install the lightning protector onto the equipment. It was February 2000, and the thunderstorm season was just two months away. The problem was, the lightning protectors were still on the production line and hadn't been assembled yet.

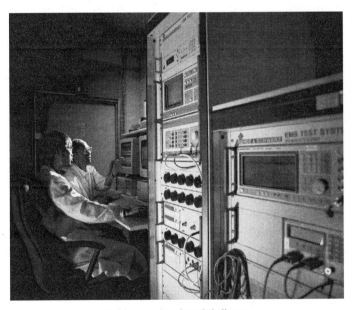

Tackling tough technical challenges

One day, during a meeting, our manager Chen Dunli received a call from the product line informing us that the shipping date had been confirmed. They wanted to know where our lightning protectors were. Mr Chen became so worried that he slammed his hand down on the table and shouted: "Get me a car! We're going to the production floor ourselves!" I was flabbergasted. "What do you mean we're going to the production floor?" I asked. Before I had a chance to digest the situation, I found myself in a Shenzhen factory with Mr Chen and two other colleagues.

We had done something
no one else in the industry
had dared to imagine.

No one knew the lightning protectors better than we did. We didn't need training before jumping right into our new roles. We sat on the production line, welding the lightning protection circuits into the boxes. The work wasn't technical, but it took us R&D guys what seemed like forever just to get a single box finished. The workers around us finished four or five boxes in the same amount of time. I looked up at Mr Chen and saw him carefully focused on the assembly work. He was more devoted to the work than anyone else, and didn't even stop for a meal. The factory manager was impressed when he saw us there: "You engineers really are workaholics," he said, "coming down here to work with us!"

After three or four days, however, it wasn't clear that our efforts were paying off, and our arms and hands were sore as hell. Nonetheless, by being there onsite, we put the manufacturer under some pressure, and they arranged for additional shifts to speed things up. This helped push things forward.

Once the lightning protectors were sent to field offices and assembled onto equipment, they did their job well. Damage caused to products from lightning strikes was reduced considerably.

A 'One vs Many' challenge

After having gotten a taste of how tough it was to try to 'patch up holes,' we no longer wanted to just be putting out fires and patching leaks. We wanted to get involved in the earlier stages of product development and incorporate lightning protection into design from the very beginning. We were still the same old team, and each of us was assigned to a different product line to lend support.

When I say 'to lend support,' I actually mean 'to spark conflicts and cause trouble.' Each product line expressed their support for our request, but implementation was a problem. We had to prove our worth to the product lines.

Not long after taking on work relating to wireless product lightning protection, a new product that had been installed with a lightning protector was damaged during a lightning strike. The head of the product line was all frowns, and questioned me: "Don't you have strict testing of the protectors? They seem to be useless.

Why don't you get it right first, then come back and talk to me about involvement in early stage design?"

When I got onsite to inspect, I found that the location of the lightning protector was entirely wrong. The grounding plan was also not appropriate, which was why it hadn't done its job properly to protect the equipment. Despite this, my explanation failed to win the trust of the product line: "Do you have any evidence to prove that? If we make the adjustments you are suggesting, do you realize how much that will affect the product engineering plan?"

Without having resolved the problem, I left dejectedly. This was not the right way to solve the issue. Perhaps a comparison might help persuade them? I thought I might present a series of differently configured lightning protectors, and let the members of the product line team see for themselves whether I was right. I analysed the effects of the lightning circuitry in detail. After multiple adjustments and optimizations, I then sought out other experts to see if my train of thought was making sense. With over 40 pages of documentation, the wireless product line engineers were quickly convinced: "Oh! So it really is that problem!" They immediately joined me in convincing the product line leadership, and got down to work adjusting the product engineering plans.

However, that wasn't the end of the battle. During the course of plan execution, we had trouble reaching consensus with the product hardware and architecture teams. In terms of the architecture, I repeatedly emphasized that lightning protectors had to be installed inside the cabinet next to the board in order to be effective. But the architecture team couldn't comprehend this: "Just put it inside. There is only so much space there. It's not going to fit." "But if we don't put it in this location, the lightning protection performance will suffer." "Give us proof of that!"

All I could do was return to the lab and prepare a series of test results with the protector in different locations. I used those results to explain my approach, one step at a time, to the architecture engineers, and eventually was able to convince them. During plan implementation, the entire process seemed to be fraught with one such battle after another.

Finally, the properly installed lightning protectors showed their value during the stormy season, and rates of damage and loss were reduced to basically zero. The lightning protection team's technical capabilities were finally recognized by the product lines.

Lightning protection: Are you willing to play with fire?

With the advent of distributed base stations, RRUs were installed on towers to reduce signal loss and cut network construction costs. This presented size-related challenges. Teams working on radio frequency and power supplies were all eager to push for their products to be part of RRUs. However, our lightning protection circuits were too large, and hindered the process of miniaturization. During one review meeting, an RRU architect said bluntly: "Everyone's circuitry is just barely squeezing onto the highway, and your lightning protection circuit is sitting in the middle of the road like a 1970s Buick sedan."

We didn't have much to say in our defense; lightning protectors hadn't seen any major breakthroughs in the past few years, so how could we achieve miniaturization? The team brainstormed again and again, analysing the feasibility of each possible component miniaturization. We eventually came up with seven potential designs. Unfortunately, each of these met with failure.

Ideas continued to fly, but then got quickly rebutted. The plan wasn't moving forward. Had we really reached the limit? "Perhaps we should give Component G a try," suggested Wang Qinghai. Using this component could achieve a circuit that was half the size of a traditional component, but there was a serious risk: other lightning protectors would automatically shut off after responding to the power surge from a strike, thus ensuring that the RRU and the lightning protector itself were both protected. Component G took up all the energy of the lightning strike itself in order to protect the other equipment and circuits. The adjustment of its voltage was a major technical challenge. If the voltage was too high, Component G wouldn't protect against the lightning. If it was too low, it could erroneously respond to DC power and damage the protector and the RRU. More frustrating than that was the fact that the voltage would constantly change based on the lightning strike.

When the manufacturers heard our 'striking' idea, they weren't even willing to entertain the possibility. "Let's just leave it for now and look into things more," they told us. Some of them even called us wishful thinkers: "This plan of yours is like playing with fire on your power circuit!" However, this was the most feasible of all of the 'impossible' plans. If this route wasn't possible, then maybe our process of miniaturization really had reached its limit.

Perhaps it is a sense of technical intuition I've gained over many years, but I never believe fate deals us an impossible hand. I decided to give my all, and tried every single wave form of lightning strike, seeking to find the most appropriate voltage for various conditions through trial and error. As the 'elder' of the team, even though I had butterflies in my stomach, I didn't let it show. Otherwise, the younger colleagues under me might have lost faith. I carried my own weight while also encouraging the younger experts. "The next wave is going to throw us onto the beach sooner or later," I assured them. "Just give everything you've got, and let fate handle the rest!"

We began to constantly look over our own work and ideas and make adjustments. First were the component feasibility assessments, then the simulations, and then the design, and finally the sample units. In order to find that critical point, each time we validated an electrical performance parameter, we would test the voltage one volt at a time. With each adjustment, we had to re-optimize the design, change the circuitry, make new samples … and then upend everything and start again. In this way, each round of design and sample creation lasted for a continuous two or three months.

Throughout this process, testing and validation were our constant companions. There were upwards of 50 or 60 components that had to be incorporated into each round of testing, and each component had to undergo at least 10 simulated lightning strikes. More than 2,000 data groups were created in each round. After several months of testing, our ears felt like they were buzzing, and we felt hazy and dizzy. After a high-voltage lightning strike test, the buzzing in our ears would generally last until we went to bed that evening.

Each round of testing was conducted full of hope, and then met with disappointment. Then a new flame of hope would ignite, with another subsequent disappointment. We spent a tortuously long time in this repetitive cycle. Finally, after six rounds of sample creation and testing, luck found us. We hit upon the optimal solution for all conditions.

In that instant, as I held the data in my hands, my throat constricted and I wasn't able to get a word out. The joyous, exciting scene I had imagined in my mind over and over again did not occur. But, the size of our lightning protector was cut by half, and we left the competition in the dust once again. We had done something no one else in the industry had dared to imagine.

Seizing real lightning

After the excitement had faded, we were surprised to discover that we had been pushed into what Huawei founder and CEO Ren Zhengfei likes to call 'uncharted territory.' With our new solution, it was no longer possible to rely on the lightning protection specifications we had used in the past. We had to find real lightning in order to obtain the most precise data. This was the only way for us to check whether the simulation modules were appropriate and accurate, and to further optimize the lightning protector.

But how could we 'seize' actual lightning? Rocket-triggered lightning! This daring idea was proposed by someone on the team. It was something only three or four organizations were doing globally, and it was mostly for meteorological research or national defense. No one in the ICT industry had ever proposed doing it, but the data from this method was the most precise, and it was thus simply irresistible to us!

In 2010, we hit it off immediately with the Guangdong Provincial Meteorological Bureau, and this marked the start of the rocket-triggered lightning project. Pulling along the power and battery cabinets, several of us squeezed into the cabin of a truck and rode the whole bumpy way to the Outdoor Lightning Detection Base of the Chinese Academy of Meteorological Science.

In our normal work we were always worried about lightning strikes damaging our equipment. But now, we found ourselves intentionally looking for lightning, and we realized it was tougher to find than we'd imagined. When we got word of inclement weather, we rushed to the location as quickly as we could, but in many cases the storm clouds had already passed when we arrived. We rushed back and forth between the base and the launch site many times a day. Sometimes we finally had the weather we were looking for, but then the rain was too heavy, and the test tower was at risk of being directly struck by lightning. This made it impossible for us to climb the tower to install the test battery, so we again had to return empty-handed.

Adjusting and testing the rocket-triggered lightning test equipment

The Outdoor Lightning Detection Base at the Lightning Protection Centre of Guangdong Province – the weather forecast showed that the next day there would be thunderstorms, so we spent the night constructing an artificial lightning attraction environment

With all eyes on the calendar, we watched as the stormy season began to pass without giving us the opportunity we needed. The weather remained sunny and hot. On 3 September there was light rain, and I was waiting for the call as usual at 6 am. Everyone had their eyes glued to the radar and electric field diagrams. By 8 am, there still wasn't the right mix of conditions to trigger lightning. But suddenly, the satellite cloud map showed that a layer of cloud was about to pass over the base. The research staff from the Meteorological Bureau called out, "Get ready to go!" We once again found ourselves racing along the road to the base in the midst of a storm. A dozen or so of us were squeezed into the tiny 'Rocket Control Room,' dripping wet, with hearts fluttering between hope and discouragement, wondering which it would be that day.

By 9 pm, we had been sitting there for over 10 hours. Everyone was staring intently at the radar and electrical field maps, ready to pull out their hair in excitement. We watched with growing exhilaration as the intensity of the electrical fields in the cloud layer grew. "Prepare for launch. Three, two, one, ignite!" The rocket carved a path through the air like a sword being brandished from its sheath, heading toward the clouds. Half a moment later, multiple blinding streaks of lightning shot down onto the tower, leaving us all awestruck and lost for words. I don't know who first shouted out, but after that everyone broke into cheers. We had finally captured lightning and successfully guided the electricity onto our communications tower, obtaining extremely valuable raw data. I had seen on television the expressions of joy among scientists working on rocket launch projects, and at that moment I also knew that incredible sense of joy.

After 'chasing lightning' for 18 years, we gradually transitioned from studying lightning protection products to studying lightning itself. Today, whether it be torrential rain or thunder and lightning, the effects of such phenomena no longer cause major disturbances to communications, and people are able to make calls to relatives far away, and chat with friends by video across oceans ... anytime, anywhere. Behind these everyday activities is our team, and our tireless effort expended over a decade, never admitting defeat, and always testing the limits of what is possible. As I bid farewell to my youth and look back on things, I can proudly say that I have no regrets.

15

Huawei Built Me a Research Lab

By Renato Lombardi

Huawei: A new chapter in a long career

One day in late 2007, Denis Han from Huawei's microwave team (who was later appointed director of the Milan Research Centre) called and asked me to meet with him.

I had first heard about Huawei three years earlier, when I was working for Siemens, and we sold Huawei some microwave equipment for a project they were doing in Cambodia. Soon afterwards, I had the opportunity to visit Huawei's headquarters in Shenzhen, the exhibition hall in the F1 building, and the manufacturing centre. I was briefed on Huawei's history and my first reaction was, "This is not just a Chinese company." Huawei had very few people working on manufacturing; R&D staff made up a huge proportion of its workforce so that it could focus on long-term innovation and development. After I came back to Siemens, I delivered an internal report, telling everyone that although Huawei was still small as a multinational company, we would see a lot from it in the coming months and years.

That brief encounter with Huawei was like a first date that ultimately led to my happy marriage with the company. But, after I visited Huawei's HQ, I didn't have any further contact with the company until I got the phone call from Denis Han.

The meeting took place just before Christmas, at a café in Milan. Alex Cai, who was the director of Huawei's European Research Institute, came along to interview me. But instead of a job interview, it was more like a business planning meeting. Alex talked frankly. He said that Huawei was not yet able to manufacture the outdoor units (ODUs) that were the centrepiece of the company's suite of microwave products for IP networks. The products they were importing were not competitive, and they lacked talented people. They were looking for microwave experts to help them develop their own ODUs and identify where microwave was moving. The company was committed to becoming a competitive player in IP microwave, and turning Huawei into a microwave brand name.

Renato Lombardi at the opening of the Microwave R&D Competence Centre

We spent the whole afternoon talking, and agreed that Huawei needed to establish its own microwave R&D competence centre. And, we concurred, the centre should be built where there were a large number of talented people, who were the key to success.

We had the same idea: Milan, the de facto home of microwave. Many famous companies – such as Siemens, Alcatel-Lucent and Ericsson – have R&D and sales departments there. There are also universities, like the Polytechnic University of Milan, which specifically train people in microwave technology. So, we could benefit a lot from the local resource pool, and a complete ecosystem of companies, schools and research institutes.

We even discussed the outlines of a plan: how many people, how much money, how much time, and so on. That meeting really excited me, and I finally made up my mind to quit my job with a Western company and go to work with Huawei.

I knew that I would perhaps be in a lower-level position at Huawei, and it would be very difficult to leave a familiar place – where I had worked for over a decade – and start over again without my existing relationships and resources. But, I have always seen myself as a man of passion, ready for all kinds of new things. I could start a new life at Huawei, build my own team and try new things. What could be more exciting than that? It would be a sort of rebirth, like closing one chapter and opening a new one. (By the way, my name Renato means 'rebirth' in Latin.)

Cutting corners, and starting with a bang

We had an interesting time building the Microwave Division.

In the summer of 2008, a group of five people assembled in a small office in one corner of Huawei's Italy Office, right next to the coffee machine. The group consisted of Denis Han, Logos Tao (who was the manager of the ODU Product Development Team in Xi'an), William Gou, Franco Marconi and me. The air-conditioner was broken and the office was noisy, but we envisioned our future there: renting an office, hiring the right people, and building a competence centre from scratch. It was this vision that kept us going through the boiling summer.

I made use of every opportunity to let people in the microwave communications industry know about Huawei and the resources it was putting into microwave. I first sought out former colleagues, who were all experts with 10–20 years of experience. We knew and trusted each other, and this was how I formed the original core team.

While we were establishing the competence centre, Huawei was facing critical business challenges. In October 2008, after the company won the bid for Vodafone's project, we came under great pressure to develop products fast. Vodafone requested that we deliver a prototype that could pass their proof of concept test within just a few months.

I prepared to build a test environment with my Chinese colleagues. But, where should it be? The new offices in Milan were just finished, and there were no laboratories yet. Huawei already had a mobile innovation lab in Spain, so most of my colleagues preferred Spain, but I insisted on doing the testing in Milan. I wanted to show the customer how committed and competitive Huawei's microwave expert team in Milan was. I thought that was the way to build a long-term relationship with the customer. In the end, we succeeded in establishing a joint innovation centre in Milan.

What I did next was a little irregular, but it's better to ask for forgiveness than permission. I had lunch with some customers at Vodafone whom I knew very well, and I said, "Next week, you'll have an official meeting with Huawei. Please ask Huawei to do the testing in Milan." A week later, they told me, "Renato, you may not know this yet, but Vodafone has asked Huawei to do the tests in Milan."

I was very excited to hear this news. However, much to my surprise, the customer set the date for the proof of concept test on the day before the Chinese Spring Festival (25 January 2009). There were only a few weeks left, so we had to build the lab very quickly.

Hu Bin, the testing engineer, brought a dozen people from China to Milan to help us out. I remember that one weekend, I was basically working as a kind of carpenter, along with the other Italians in the team, laying the tiles in the lab. We did things that researchers don't normally do, like flooring and wiring. We saw the Microwave Division as our home, so everyone was very committed. We knew this was a pivotal moment and we had to start with a bang. Everyone was so dedicated that nobody had a problem coming in during the weekends.

We managed to build the lab from scratch within two weeks. Nonetheless, the deadline for the test came before the product had gotten to the important TR4 milestone.

Our Chinese colleagues in Xi'an and Chengdu gave up the chance to spend the holidays with their families in order to support us 24/7. Every day, after conducting the tests for the customer, the teams in Milan, Xi'an and Chengdu worked into the small hours to identify problems and make improvements, modify the code and compile new versions, and conduct many rounds of tests and verification.

That was when I came to realize the true meaning of dedication (*fendou*) and the values that inspire everyone at Huawei to keep forging ahead.

The tests hit a few road bumps, and were not perfect, but thanks to the concerted efforts of all the teams, we finally reached the customer's required standards about two weeks later. A few days later, Ryan Ding, at the time president of Huawei's Fixed Network Product Line, came to Milan. I explained to Mr Ding why we chose to do the test in Milan, but I was a bit worried, because I had cut some corners. "Don't worry," he said. "Because of your involvement, Huawei had decided to do the test in Milan – even before you asked. And it proved to be the right decision."

This was just the beginning, but it meant a lot to us. This was the first time we had demonstrated Huawei's own microwave technology to a key customer. We proved to the customer that Huawei

Milan possessed not only R&D and design capabilities, but we also had technical sales and services capabilities, and were able to build relationships with customers. We deeply understood and met the customer's needs, and delivered on them. Just as a car needs fuel to run, I needed to do the tests in Milan.

Lombardi demonstrates innovations to the customer

When faced with two options, sometimes you have to start laying the groundwork in advance, instead of waiting till the last minute to make a choice. Actually, Italians don't mind cutting corners, just like the Chinese. If there is an obstacle, I just go around it to reach my target. If we are absolutely forced to meet the obstacle head on, then we just try our best to overcome it.

A two-year challenge, completed in one year

By the second half of 2008, the Microwave Division in Milan had already taken shape. The in-house R&D of ODUs was then brought to the table.

Our ODUs were made by a partner company, and they were not competitive in terms of performance, technology and overall quality. They didn't match up to the offerings of incumbent manufacturers in the field. Drawing on my more than 20 years of experience, I proposed a solution of just a single board during my first trip to our research centre in Chengdu. This solution would surpass the two-board designs offered by our competitors in terms of performance and production capacity. But, it would also increase technical difficulty, putting more pressure on our R&D teams.

Some people supported this new solution, but others didn't. My team members and I strongly believed in this approach, and tried to persuade other teams to go for it with us. After a long period of phone calls and emails back and forth, I decided to fly with other microwave experts from Milan to Xi'an, because the Xi'an Research Centre was just approved to be the new home of ODU development in China. I wanted to talk face-to-face with the R&D team of the Wireless Network Product Line.

It was a freezing morning. A few people, including Logos Tao and me, wandered along the ancient city walls in the chilly wind for a long time. As we walked, we tried to analyse the strengths and weaknesses of the old solution and the new one. We also thought about possible problems with the new solution, either in technology or structure. I said to Logos, "We're confident that we can build this new solution. The industry doesn't believe that Huawei can make an ODU prototype within two years. We'll prove to them that we can do it in one year."

Our discussion with the R&D team there lasted a good four hours. Though we all knew that there was some risk in taking this new technical path, we insisted on our choice.

About a year later, in 2009, we succeeded. We built an ODU prototype and officially released our own microwave product. My team had made good on its commitment! The product was named the XMC series, which stood for eXtreme Modulation Capacity. I immediately realized that XMC was short for Xi'an, Milan and Chengdu, and it represented the joint innovation and development efforts of the three teams.

Commitment to ambitious goals is the best motivation

Many challenges lay ahead as we tried to develop industry-leading microwave products. The design of super-high-frequency circuits for millimetre wave had long been recognized as a tough nut to crack. So, we decided that for the E-band board, it was important to have the R&D team and the manufacturing team in the same place. Standard practice was to have the two work relatively independently, but on such a high-frequency board, even a tiny problem could have catastrophic consequences. We had to consider all potential manufacturing problems during the design process, while ensuring a reasonable profit margin. If the board was manufactured in China, there would be a number of technical difficulties, and we were having trouble importing some of the key components there. In the end, we all agreed that part of the 80 GHz board should be manufactured in Milan.

I found a consultant in Milan with considerable experience and expertise in manufacturing microwave products. With his help, the R&D team learned about the manufacturing process and key control points, which were critical to product quality assurance. We managed to increase the capacity of high frequency system-in-a-package (SIP), and then ship it back to our Chinese factory to be installed in the product.

Since we had never developed an E-band product before, we spent a few months with the production line, doing tests and verifications to solve problems.

Over that period, the E-band expert team worked day and night, tirelessly conducting experiments and solving problems. At one point, a new problem occurred, causing a drop in our production capacity. So, a group of us travelled to our manufacturing facility in Songshan Lake, where we worked with the teams from Xi'an, Chengdu and Shanghai to identify the root cause. I still remember that trip to China, because I had broken my arm playing basketball back home, and I had to wear a cast the whole time.

Much to our delight, we solved every problem we encountered. We built a leading position in the microwave industry, and we now have the largest global market share.

Culture is all about adaptation

Over the past eight years, I have often been asked the same question. As a Westerner working for a Chinese company, how do you adapt to the different culture?

I don't think this is anything special. Although big companies have different management systems, they all share certain qualities. We just need to understand how to work in a big company.

Many non-Chinese managers at Huawei Europe have previously worked at the headquarters of big companies, such as Ericsson and Siemens. They often come to me to seek advice on how to communicate with people at Huawei. I usually suggest that they change their approach, because they haven't really understood that they are not in the company headquarters any more (the HQ is in China). No matter where you are, you need to adapt to the new company's values, the leaders, their way of working and their management style. You have to find how you can contribute.

You also need to learn about China and Huawei, and understand their culture and way of thinking, so as to better communicate with your colleagues. I first visited China 25 years ago, and travelled around many of the country's provinces. Wherever I went, I would take a tour, visit the scenic spots, and go to restaurants to try the local specialities. Gradually, I found myself falling in love with China, Chinese culture and Chinese history.

I often tell the non-Chinese experts in my team to learn some basic Chinese, and to not always insist on eating Italian food, or going to fast food joints or other Western restaurants. When you're in China, eat the food, because this is the way we can better understand our Chinese colleagues. Many of my Chinese colleagues ask me, "Can you speak Chinese?" I cannot actually speak the language, but I have learned about 300 to 400 Chinese characters, and those have been a very valuable tool for me.

Lombardi and customers discuss the prototype built in Milan

Understanding a person is way more important than speaking a language. Charles Darwin told us a long time ago that it is not the strongest who will survive, but those who adapt to a new environment quickly.

Culture is all about adapting and respecting diversity. No one expects me to behave exactly like a Chinese person. As an Italian, I deeply respect China's culture and its people. Perhaps this is the reason why my Chinese colleagues so often choose to forgive and accept my mistakes!

"Always look on the bright side"

How can we better adapt to a new environment? Personally speaking, I try to complain less and smile more, and always look on the bright side.

Eight years ago, Huawei was like a child, not yet in its teens. Though it was big, it was not mature in many ways. This was especially true of the processes and management systems. Some colleagues used to complain a lot, and they would even ask me, "How come you never get angry?" I used to say, "We were hired to identify problems, propose suggestions and solve the problems. All companies have problems as they grow, and Huawei is no exception. If there were no problems, then why would we be here?"

I had a hard time fitting in here at first. But Huawei managers, especially senior executives, gave me a lot of support – in a way that I had never experienced before. Their support gave me confidence, and helped me find the best way to work with teams at HQ and in other locations.

I remember my first visit to Shenzhen after joining the company. I met senior executives, and they asked me, "How can we support you?" This was really impressive, because in most companies, you usually only meet senior executives to submit a report. Two hours after my meeting with the leadership, I started receiving calls from other colleagues who had been assigned to support me. I was deeply impressed by their leadership and ability to get things done. After that, every time I visited Shenzhen, I would send an email to various executives, and they would set aside some time to talk with me. At the end of each conversation, they would always ask, "How can I support you?"

A company cannot grow, improve or change overnight. It takes time, and we need to be understanding. As long as we are heading in the right direction, we can be patient and wait for certain things to fall into place. It's like climbing a mountain. We may be attacked by mosquitoes along the way, but we shouldn't stop climbing. We should kill them and move on, because our target is to climb to the top.

"I'm a wolf, too"

More than one Chinese colleague has said to me, "You are very Huawei." And I do think my character matches very well with Huawei's values.

When I'm in Milan, I arrive at the research lab early and leave late. After dinner with my family, I turn on my laptop and continue working. That is my life, every day, regular as clockwork. In addition, I spend about 140 days travelling around the world every year, most often to China. Wherever I am, on a plane or a train, I set up my laptop to work. I'm always thinking. As soon as I have an idea, I write it down. I love this job, and I have never drawn a distinction between my life and work, because work has always been a part of my life.

All the other microwave team members are similarly dedicated. There are now 50 people in the team. I don't check up on their work, because I trust my team, and I don't want to micromanage them. Everyone must take responsibility for their own work. If something needs to be done, you will do your utmost to get it done.

I like showing people my staff card. I tell them, "My employee ID is 900004, which means I was the fourth non-Chinese employee in the European Research Institute, and I was also the first non-Chinese employee in the Microwave Division in Milan." It's a nice reminder. I'm often the only non-Chinese employee present at meetings in China. I have worked at Huawei for many years now, and the moment I decided to join the company I made up my mind not to go halfway.

Lombardi's lanyards from many technology conferences

To this day, I still see myself as a lucky guy. I'm very lucky because I get to work with an excellent team, conduct industry-leading research, and contribute new thoughts and ideas. The Microwave Division in Milan started from nothing and has been growing ever since. It is like my baby, and it has become a part of my life. Looking to the future, I see many opportunities awaiting us.

Someone once said to me that to work at Huawei you need to be aggressive like a wolf. So, it's a good thing that I'm a wolf, too – I love to eat raw meat. (Just kidding!) I see both Italians and Chinese as pragmatists. No matter where we are from, as long as we can make the things everyone needs, the world will open its arms to us.

16

From Luck to Skill:
The Story of
the Mate Series

By Li Xiaolong

The Mate series is one of Huawei's most successful lines of phones. But, not many people know the background. At the start, this series was mired in many setbacks and difficulties. A lot of people doubted that it would ever be a success. Yet, we stuck to one principle: target the most pressing needs of our customers as precisely as we can. This principle was built into the DNA of the Mate series. We were sure that if we followed this principle, the Mate would be a success. All we needed was time and opportunity. And over the last five years, the Mate has been welcomed by consumers. Of course, there have been some challenges along the way, and I'd like to share some of those stories with you.

Huawei needs a flagship phone

This story is about the Mate, but I have to start with the P1. For Huawei, and for me, the P1 was the company's 'Zero to One' moment. It was our first flagship smartphone under the Huawei brand. Before the P1, we had always produced phones in association with operators. Now, we were building our own high-end brand name. This was a watershed in the history of Huawei's Consumer Business Group.

In 2011, Huawei only sold low-end and mid-range phones, and we were still making feature phones. Richard Yu had just been appointed CEO of the Huawei Consumer Business Group, and he proposed that we build our own flagship smartphone. I had been in charge of feature phones, but my manager asked me to move from Xi'an to Shanghai to lead the development of our first flagship smartphone. As soon as I got off the plane in Shanghai, the first thing I did was buy a flagship phone made by every one of our competitors, so I could get an idea of what was on the market. At the time, my team and I had very limited experience with smartphones. The last smartphone I had bought for my own personal use had run the Windows Mobile operating system. Android was still a new platform at the time, and I knew nothing about it.

We quickly reached out to all the other Huawei teams who designed smartphones and learned what we could from them. Once we had a basic idea about how to build these products, we started to plan Huawei's first venture into the space, the P1. At the time, our thinking was simple: benchmark our phone against those our competitors already had on the market, use leading technology for each function, and give our customers the best possible experience in every area. So, we selected the very best solutions for the phone's form factor, processor, operating system, memory, camera, interior components and battery. In terms of the structural design, we packed the most advanced components as closely as possible. The P1 had more new components than any other Huawei phone at that time, and it was much harder to develop than we had imagined. By the time the P1 hit the shelves, it was considerably over-budget.

In 2012, we finally launched the P1 onto the market, with great expectations. Since it was powered by leading technology, we expected it to be a bestseller. Unfortunately, the market's response was a slap in the face. Our global sales were only a few hundred thousand units, nowhere near what our competitors achieved, and significantly worse than the sales of Huawei's own low-end and mid-range phones.

From hope to hopeless … we were left consoling ourselves with poor excuses. "It was just our first attempt." "At least we tested the waters." But, we obviously had to look back at what had really gone wrong. When you make a phone, you cannot just pursue high performance. Just putting all of the most advanced technologies into one phone is no guarantee of success. You need expertise in a whole range of other areas, for example, branding. We set the price of the P1 at ¥2,999, making it the most expensive Chinese-made phone on the market. Unfortunately, our customers still thought of Huawei phones as freebies that their broadband providers handed out when they signed a contract. Most people simply weren't ready to pay ¥3,000 for a Huawei phone.

Another example: retail expertise. The P1 was one of our first forays into the retail market. We had previously only sold directly to operators. Most retailers had little interest in working with us, because our brand was not attractive at that time. Today, you can see the Huawei logo everywhere, but that was not the case back then. We never managed to get the P1 shelf space in either Gome or Suning, China's two biggest electronics retail chains. In 2012, our company's Consumer Business Group started mobilizing its employees to go out and personally promote Huawei phones in stores. I found that the stores I was assigned to didn't even sell the product. It was a humbling moment.

Despite the problems, we had learned many lessons from this process. Huawei's flagship smartphones had set sail, and everyone kept their eyes on the future and the successes to come.

A product to keep us going

Those successes took longer than any of us had imagined. For close to a year, we launched a series of high-end phones, and each time met with crushing defeat. It seemed like the harder we tried, the worse we did. The team was in trouble, and morale sank through the floor. "Why can't we get this right?" we kept wondering, as the frustration continued. It was also hitting us personally. So long as our phones were losing money, there was nothing in the bonus pot for my team.

We needed a product that could sustain our operations. With these revised expectations in mind, we started the development of the Mate 1. The trend at that time was for screens to get fractionally bigger each year. We thought, can't we just skip to the end of this process and design a phone that has the largest possible screen, while staying small enough to hold in the hand? The other big issue with smartphones was battery life. There were no phones with massive screens and super-long charge cycles, so we focused on those two issues. We planned to make a 6.1-inch screen, which would be our unique selling point. For the other functions and specifications, all we wanted was to make sure they didn't let our customers down. We'd go with tried-and-tested components, and minimize our costs.

When the product rolled off the production line, both the online and offline sales teams wanted to sell it, because the big screen was a great selling point. It gave them something to work with. However, both teams were also somewhat hesitant, because none of our previous phones had performed well. With no one quite ready to commit, management made the decision: we would make two different editions, with different amounts of memory, and they would be sold by both teams. Unfortunately, coordination between the teams was not easy. One team wanted one tagline, the other team preferred another slogan, and it took a lot of meetings to get every-one on the same page. During the process, we made some mistakes in our stock projections. So, when sales took off, we didn't have enough units in stock. By the time we had stocked up, the phone had stopped selling.

Huawei phones only sold in small numbers back then, so even though the first Mate phone did not sell a huge number of units, for us, it was a success. Unfortunately, we had a lot of excess materials (mainly the batteries and screens, because of their long production lead times), and that waste devoured all of our profits.

We had warehouses full of screens and batteries. We had to find a way to use them up. So, the development of the Mate 2 was really forced upon us. Our selling point would once again be the big screen, but this time we fitted the phone with Huawei's first-gen-eration system-on-a-chip, the Kirin 910. It was designed for 4G networks, and it was ahead of any other chip the industry had to offer. But, the Mate 2 was not attractive enough as a whole package, and, as before, sales were lukewarm. With two generations under its belt, the Mate series was just about staying out of the red, but it hadn't delivered any real profits.

What we didn't realize at the time was that these two Mate phones, with moderate sales, had paved the way for our future success. Smartphones universally suffered from short battery lives, and the Mate 1 and Mate 2 had managed to combine a large screen with a long-lasting battery. Customers loved it, and we were starting to build a following of Mate fans. These admirers had a very distinctive user profile, and their needs helped us set our direction as we developed the Mate 7, which was destined to be our breakout product.

Here's one for the fans …

At one of our meetings in 2013, an industrial designer showed us a new design for a phone that made me very excited. It was an all-metal body with a huge screen, and it looked both elegant and understated. I said to myself, "This is the product that I want." It became the prototype design for the Mate 7, from which we planned the next Mate phone.

As mentioned, the Mate 1 and Mate 2 may not have been financial blockbusters, but they did give us a much more valuable asset: a group of committed Mate fans. Our customer surveys gave us a clear picture of these consumers: they were often elite professionals, with a measured level of success; they had some experience of the good life, and their careers were on an upward trajectory. But, they also had many responsibilities – children, elderly parents, mortgages, car loans, etc.

What did they want from a mobile phone? They used their phones for work as well as for leisure, so they preferred a bigger screen. They were heavy users, so battery life was extremely important. They liked the Mate because of the large screen and the long-lasting battery, so it was vital that we kept these two strengths. Their phones were necessary tools for their work, so high performance was essential. The large screen meant that we would need a compact design, with a high screen-to-body ratio, and it would need to look solid and serious to suit a person of status and importance.

Armed with this user information, the project to build the next phone, codenamed Jazz, began. To achieve the high performance that we wanted, we decided to use Huawei's latest Kirin chip at the time, the 920. This was the first time our processors would have a real edge over the competition. To maintain smaller dimensions, we racked our brains for ways to pack the components together. At one point, we even considered putting the camera at the bottom of the phone, to shave 2 mm off the length. But if we had gone through with it, our phone users would have been shooting selfies from underneath their chins, and would have squashed faces in every picture. This was hardly the experience we wanted our users to have, so we dropped the idea.

We also added a completely new function with a fingerprint scanner that could unlock the phone. Today, this is nothing major, but five years ago this function did not exist on any phone on the market, and there were no fingerprint chipsets available off the shelf. Back then, the iPhone 5s had not yet been launched, and other phones with fingerprint scanners first required a button-press, then a swipe. The inclusion of this new function was one of our biggest internal controversies.

"It's a white elephant! It's expensive, and it bulks up the phone for no added value!"

"It's so practical! This function is going to send the phone flying off the shelves!"

The row went on and on. I supported the fingerprint function. I talked about this situation: imagine you've been working all day, you're tired, and you want to call your family – your parents, or your wife and children. The last thing you want to do is enter a password to unlock your phone.

A little story like this is not a magic spell. It didn't persuade everyone straight away. But, in the end, we decided to include the fingerprint function – a decision that led directly to the next controversy: whether we put it on the front or the back of the phone. I was adamant that the scanner should go on the back of the phone, because in a phone with a big screen, the form factor is crucial. A fingerprint scanner could be embedded into the back of the phone without increasing the dimensions, and it would also be the right place for our customers. In the end, the market proved that this was the right decision. The rear-mounted fingerprint scanner became one of the phone's most celebrated features.

Of course, the Mate 7 was not a perfect phone. Cost considerations prevented us from using the very best components for every part. We listed out the cost of the phone item by item, and were uncompromising in what we decided to eliminate. Every time we removed something, it hurt, but it was necessary. In the end, we couldn't spend much on the camera. At the time, we didn't think our customers would be that interested in the camera function.

So, function by function and feature by feature, we finalized the design and the specifications of the phone. Unlike the first two Mate phones, we had complete clarity on what we wanted to achieve with this product. We had to respond to each one of the needs of our target consumers, and, in the end, we were fully confident in our product.

When we got together to decide on the marketing strategy, a lot of people said that it would be a mistake to call this phone the Mate 3. Neither the Mate 1 nor Mate 2 had sold well, so the wholesalers and retailers were not particularly confident in the Mate series. Continuing with the Mate name might lead to poor sales. There was a proposal to call this the D series, and another to call it the X. By the end of the meeting we decided that the phone would be called the D7. It looked like the end of the Mate line, but after the meeting I went and lobbied the executives to keep the name. My reason was simple: Mate is a friend, and this was a phone you could rely on.

You didn't have to worry about its battery running down, or about the system glitching. You could feel relaxed, because this was your loyal friend. After we had talked it through, we gave the phone the name Mate 7. It's interesting to look back and think that the Mate series was very nearly 'two strikes and you're out.'

In 2014, after a difficult birth, the Mate 7 went on sale.

Official launch of the HUAWEI Mate 7 in Berlin

Large crowds at the HUAWEI Mate 7 launch event

A well-planned, but unexpected, blockbuster

"Xiaolong, how many units do you think the Mate 7 is going to ship?" a colleague from another team asked me, soon before the phone hit the shelves.

I said 1.2 million but, to be honest, I was stretching. If we could sell eight or nine hundred thousand, it would have been a big win for us. In terms of technology, the Mate 7 was a cutting-edge phone. And in order to sell a lot of phones, you need a top-quality product. But, we had experienced too many failures to think that this was enough.

At the launch event, we announced the price of ¥2,999 for the standard edition and ¥3,699 for the premium edition, which was met with a shocked silence. No Chinese-made phone had ever sold for more than ¥3,000, and a lot of people thought we had made the wrong choice. They said the Huawei brand could not support a phone costing more than ¥3,000. This phone, they said, was just going to be another Mate failure.

With four months left to go in 2014, our China regional office held a meeting in Shanghai, and asked sales teams from different parts of the country how many Mate 7 phones they thought they would sell in the next four months. The leader of the team with the biggest territory in China came up onto the stage and said, "10,000." My heart sank. If our biggest sales team only wanted to take such a small shipment, they must not have seen any prospects for this product. To make things worse, other teams in the hall started calling out, "10,000? You must be joking! There's no way you'll move that many."

I also saw a blog post written by an engineer who worked on Vmall, Huawei's online store, which said they were worried about too many people logging on to buy the phone and overwhelming the servers. However, when he saw the price of the Mate 7, he felt a weight was lifted from his shoulders because, at that price, he felt there was little chance of too much traffic.

Amid all of these negative signs, I went back and reviewed our original strategy once more. First, the product did not need to be cutting edge in every way, but it had to be high quality, with some clear selling points. Second, the phone was aimed precisely at the pain points of our target customer group, and these customers were powerful brand advocates who would promote us through word-of-mouth. Third, the product and the brand needed to be well-matched, but it was OK to be a little aspirational, and our positioning was still reasonable. We hadn't tried to pose as something we couldn't justify. Fourth, with a few years' experience under our belt, Huawei's ability to sell phones was improving. We had transformed ourselves in terms of marketing, sales channels and retail capabilities.

We had run through these factors, forward and back, over and again, and we had cut the initial production run down to three months' inventory. If we did start to sell well, we could gear up production. At the same time, if sales were lower than predicted, we wouldn't be left with a massive backlog of stock. All that was left was to wait and see what would happen.

Just one week after the Mate 7 hit the shelves, we started to receive messages from across China: "The Mate 7 has sold out, send more stock." The engineer who wrote the blog post about anticipated traffic volume on the online store wrote a follow-up item, saying that the number of buyers there was rising every day, and it was starting to worry him. He was frantically adding capacity to make sure the servers didn't get paralysed by the traffic.

Two weeks after the launch, you couldn't get a Mate 7 for asking. All the retailers who previously didn't want to work with Huawei were now clamouring to be our partners. They were setting up special Huawei islands in their stores and putting our logo above their doors. Many stores that sold phones were putting up blackboards outside with 'Mate 7 in stock' on them, to pull people in. Our team members were suddenly finding themselves to be very socially desirable, with old friends and acquaintances rekindling relationships ... and asking, "Is there any chance you can help me get a Mate 7?"

Sales of the Mate 7 blew everyone's projections out of the water, including those by my team and me. This was a huge and sorely-needed confidence booster for us, and the sales figures also brought us new kinds of experience and expertise in branding, marketing, sales channel management and retailing.

The HUAWEI Mate 7 was named 2015 New Smartphone of the Year by Hurun, publisher of China's Rich List

Expanding our appeal

The Mate 7 was a hit, and now we were able to invest more resources in the Mate series. The big screen, long-lasting battery, high performance, compact design – all of these features were now firmly established as part of the DNA of a Mate phone. From the Mate 8 to the Mate 10, we followed the same pattern. We upgraded the processors, appearance, cameras and screens, so that in each iteration we were using the very best technologies available and bringing the best experience to our customers. We let our costs rise so that we could give customers the very best product. Our image improved, allowing us to position the phone as more of a premium product. Our brand grew stronger, and was able to support higher prices, helping us develop more competitive phones that deliver better experiences. This created a virtuous cycle of improvement.

In particular, I want to mention the Mate 9 Pro, which had the smallest screen of any Mate phone, at just 5.5 inches. Many people asked why we would abandon the large screen. Wasn't it a key selling point of the Mate? But we weren't just giving up on our unique selling point. Our goal was to give more people the chance to experience the inspired performance of Huawei phones.

You have to think about it in terms of customer habits. For every phone maker in the world, except Huawei, small-screen phones outsell big-screen phones. In fact, large-screen phones can be seen as a niche market. The consumer mainstream is the smaller screen. For example, in China, many female consumers find the Mate to be too big, and it doesn't fit comfortably in their hand. Mate phones have never sold very well in Western Europe, and one of the major reasons is that Europeans find the Mate screen too big. It's not what they are used to in a smartphone.

Therefore, I always had a vision of extending the reach of the Mate, and bringing the Mate experience to more users. When we were planning the Mate 9, I suggested developing the Mate 9 Pro, with a 5.5-inch screen that matched the standard size. In every other respect, it would be identical to the Mate 9: a top-of-the-range phone.

The difference between 5.9 and 5.5 inches may not sound like much, but in the world of the smartphone, where every millimetre counts, shrinking the body by 0.4 inches makes the phone much more difficult to design. To give you the simplest example, when the phone was shrunk down, the Mate 9's 4,000 mAh battery no longer fit in the case, and there was a danger that battery life would be affected. We demanded that the Mate 9 Pro achieve the smaller dimensions without impacting the specifications at all. If we couldn't give our consumers an inspired experience and a world-beating product, then we might as well give them nothing at all. So, our battery team got down to work and slowly, painstakingly, raised the capacity of the smaller battery from 3,700 mAh to 4,000 mAh.

As the design became more challenging, the cost went up. To fit the same components into a smaller space, the Mate 9 Pro had to use a more expensive organic light-emitting diode (OLED) screen. The Consumer Business Group's management wanted to cancel the phone on several occasions because the cost was too high, and they thought we couldn't offer it to our customers for a reasonable price.

But I stuck to my guns. I wanted the Mate 9 Pro to take us to a larger and richer group of consumers. I was willing to sacrifice some profits and accept slimmer margins. At one meeting, I joked, "We want the Mate 9 Pro to be a phone that might lose customers because of the price, but will never lose a customer because of its quality."

The retail price for the Mate 9 Pro was finally set at ¥4,699 for the standard edition and ¥5,299 for the premium edition. Personally, I don't think the value of that phone was in the money it made for us, but in the statement it made. The phone had a smaller screen, but with big-screen performance and battery life. This showed the world the strength of our R&D, and it raised our brand to another level, bringing more high-end consumers into contact with Huawei. The phone also let everyone know that the Huawei brand can support top-end phones. Our customer surveys showed that the Mate 9 Pro did attract the largest number of high-value consumers.

From the first generation of the Mate, in 2013, to today's Mate 10, the series has a history of just five years. But in that time, we have put out 10 phones in 6 generations. Some of them have been hits, and some of them have underperformed. Many complex factors can affect the success of a single phone. Sales are always a combination of skill and luck, and this is something we are still working out ourselves. Nonetheless, when I look at the entire Mate series, I can proudly say that the bit of success we have achieved today was the result of good work by our team. No matter how many times we stumbled, we always got back on our feet, and kept our eyes fixed on the ultimate goal: look, that is where our customers are.

Holding the Fort in Iceland

By Shu Jianzhen

Time passes so quickly. I had never imagined that I would spend eight years of my career at Huawei in Iceland. I have grown from a simple young man into a father. But even though I'm not young any more, my enthusiasm remains undimmed. My life in Iceland has not been very dramatic, but it has given me a store of lasting memories.

Journey to Iceland

I believe in fate. In August 2007, during my new employee orientation training, I read an essay called *Unique Iceland*, by Ren Zhengfei, founder and CEO of Huawei. I dreamed of visiting that beautiful country, perched on the edge of the Arctic Circle. After training, I was sent to a department in Changsha that develops Huawei's Business Support System (BSS). I was part of a team supporting customers outside China who use our BSS. Soon enough, I was assigned to a project in the Middle East. Just as I was applying for my passport, I was told that the project team in Iceland was short of staff, and I would have to fill in there. This marked the beginning of my work in that country.

In December 2007, not quite four months after joining Huawei, I set off on my journey to Iceland. I felt excited that my dream was finally coming true. But, I was also worried about the challenges ahead, such as the language and gaps in my technical knowledge. As we approached Iceland, the plane flew through floating clouds and blue sky. The pure, clean sky made me feel a little more relaxed.

Iceland sits close to the Arctic Circle, and Reykjavik is the northernmost capital city in the world, the only one with midnight sun and midday moon. I arrived in Iceland at 3 pm and experienced the midday moon for the first time. It was as dark as midnight.

Growing with our customer

At that time, the project in Iceland was at the Friendly User Test stage. The network had already been installed by our Chinese colleagues responsible for delivery. Now, a colleague and I took over the maintenance of a number of important elements in the network. These included the Convergent Billing System (CBS), partner relationship management system and the mediation platform.

The billing system is the core of the BSS, and also the primary source of revenue for the customer. The system we were using then was very flexible, but had a number of problems. The documentation was limited and maintenance was difficult. The customer called it a 'monster,' as it was very powerful, but hard to control. Every day, I schlepped my laptop around, dealing with issues as they arose. In order to solve problems more effectively, I used to stay up until midnight, when my colleagues back at HQ were just getting into work, so I could discuss the problems with them. For major issues, we had to spend the whole night working on them.

Once, when our project team was having a meal together, I received a phone call from the customer, complaining that some users had made payments but still could not make phone calls. I left the table immediately and asked the waiter if I could use a side room. I got the customer's permission and accessed their system using my phone as a hotspot. When I finally solved the problem, my other colleagues had already finished their meal.

Another incident occurred one Christmas, when I had just started cooking a Chinese-style duck in beer. The customer called to report a problem with the wireless integrated service gateway, saying that their users could not get online. I immediately drove to the equipment room, but forgot to turn off the gas. When I came back, the duck was burnt to a crisp. Fortunately, the oven was made of tempered glass, so at least the building did not catch fire.

On another occasion, I happened to be on vacation back in China at billing time. The customer's system experienced memory overflow and session deadlock when the customer tried to generate bills for network users. These problems could lead to delays in generating call records, and even loss of call data. I had to help work through these issues every time billing came around. Since I was back at my parents' home, with no access to broadband, I had to book a hotel in town for two days. I got the customer's permission to work on the problems remotely. Finally, I was able to help our customer produce its bills (the phone bills sent by the operator to the end users).

That was the way we worked: identifying problems and responding to them immediately. That was how we practised Huawei's core value of 'staying customer-centric.' It was sometimes painful, but the results were worth the pain. Thanks to our unflagging efforts, the customer developed more trust in Huawei, and signed a three-year contract with us to support their billing and maintenance. In 2011, the customer signed a five-year contract with us for comprehensive maintenance of their wireless network, core network and software, and renewed it at the end of 2015. By that time, Huawei was their de facto exclusive supplier.

With trust in each other, we can grow together. The customer's business has grown steadily: from a small company founded in 2007, it has now become the second largest mobile operator in Iceland. Its data business has been particularly successful – it now carries 60% of the country's mobile data. Huawei's support has been an important part of this success, but the customer's open corporate culture is another key factor. Their senior executives meet with all employees in the canteen every week, updating them on the company's progress, brainstorming solutions to problems, sharing good results and recognizing particular achievements. In this way, the company tries to encourage its employees and inspire passion.

The customer likes to take care of us, as well. They give us free office space, and often send us fruit and movie tickets. They treat us like family, and we work together toward the same goals. I have been very proud to see the customer achieve its targets, one after another, because I have played a part in their success. In June 2015, to recognize my efforts over the past eight years, the customer's chief information officer proposed naming the new CBS system 'Xiaoshu' (Shu junior), in tribute to my unborn baby.

Europe can be a hardship posting, too

Iceland is the westernmost part of Europe, and is known for its unspoiled natural beauty. One-eighth of the country's territory is covered by glaciers, and it has over 200 volcanoes. This extraordinary landscape attracts a steady flow of tourists. But, when you live there, you find that the climate really does have a cold edge to it: even in the 'hottest' months of summer, you need good, thick clothing. My colleagues used to joke that in Iceland we needed a down coat all year.

During the long, polar night of winter, there is scarcely any daylight. We can experience all four seasons in one day: from a sunny morning to a biting wind that comes off the ocean, carrying flurries of snow. The roads ice over, and it is very difficult to get about. One year, our regional vice president for project delivery came to visit a customer in Iceland, but just as he was about to leave, a blizzard closed the airport expressway and grounded all planes.

But the weather is not even the most difficult aspect of life in Iceland. Meals are a bigger problem. We don't have a canteen, so I have to cook for myself. Public transport is scarce, so I can usually only get to the stores at the weekend, and I have to battle through the wind hauling a week's worth of supplies. In the rainy season, I often look like a drowned rat by the time I get home.

There is very little food variety available in Iceland – you could count the number of different fruits and vegetables in the stores on your fingers – and prices are high. With a colleague, I once worked out what the biggest price gap was between China and Iceland, and the answer was tofu. A piece of tofu that you could buy for ¥1 in China costs ¥50 in Iceland. The Huawei housing facilities are some way from the office, so rather than go back to cook for lunch, I cook two portions each evening, one for dinner, and one for the next day's lunch. I have lived on these 'leftover lunches' for years.

Haircuts are another problem. That they are expensive goes without saying, but the small population means that hairdressers don't get much practice, either. They can manage a flat-top, but anything more complicated than that is a risk. And communication is not easy: somehow none of us in the Iceland team ever managed to quite get on the same wavelength as a barber. In the end, we brought our own hairdressing equipment from China. For several years, we used to cut each other's hair, and over time we became quite skilled – certainly the equal of any local salon! But, by 2012, I was the only Chinese guy in the office, so I had to do my best with the clippers and a mirror. I became quite handy at that, as well.

In 2008, when a senior executive came to Iceland to meet our customers, he sat down with the Chinese staff and said that he had seen how tough it was for us living here. He said we could ask for whatever we needed to make our lives easier – he would even find a way to send us for an occasional break in another country. We were touched by this concern for our wellbeing, and it inspired us to work even harder, but none of us actually took him up on the offer. I never found life in Iceland as hard as all that.

SPIRIT

With trust in each other,
we can grow together.

Holding the fort

In June 2008, the network rollout team officially handed over the complete network to our maintenance team. The customer signed a contract with Huawei for maintenance services, plus onsite operation and maintenance. Four staff members, including me, were responsible for maintaining the software system. Chen, the maintenance project manager, handled customer relations; Kang and I were on operation and maintenance; and Michel, a Polish guy, did data service maintenance.

At first, the Iceland office was quite lively. We would visit the volcanic baths, have meals together and play cards. Life was certainly not boring. Then my colleagues left, one after another. Chen was the first to leave Iceland, after less than one year working there; Michel was the second to leave. After he left, another guy named Michel joined us. He left after about half a year because he didn't like being separated from his girlfriend. Kang, the only woman in our team, managed to maintain a long-distance relationship with her boyfriend in China for five years. She eventually returned to China to be a product service engineer.

We came to realize over time that it would be very difficult to find staff from other countries willing to work long term in Iceland. We also tried hiring local engineers. We brought some in for interviews, but, ultimately, nothing came of it. The entire country has a population of just 300,000, and the working population is obviously smaller. Working in telecommunications, there is only a tiny pool of people. So, I have been stuck here for years, with no one available to replace me.

One thing I remember clearly was Lu Yong, president of Huawei's Northern & Eastern European region, coming to Iceland in May 2013 to see a customer. It was the first time I'd met him. He found out about the difficulties of working in Iceland, and our customers' high regard for my work, and has since talked about me several times. He even spoke highly of me at the regional annual meeting. I have given a lot to the company, but it has been recognized, and that makes me all the more determined and committed.

Finding love 10,000 miles away

Due to limited social connections and busy schedules, a lot of Huawei staff working abroad worry about finding and maintaining relationships. When my friends started getting married, one after another, it left me feeling a little anxious and alone.

Every time I returned to China, my family would arrange for me to meet some 'suitable prospects,' but they never seemed to work out. Perhaps fate makes arrangements for everyone. I made a friend online. We talked on and off for two years, and when we met in person, we just clicked. After I went back to Iceland, we carried on talking, often late into the night. My lonely days had come to an end.

We kept up our long-distance relationship for a few years, and in 2012 we finally got married. I felt so blessed that I had a job that I loved and a beautiful and considerate wife. But we also faced a harsh reality: we were unable to spend much time together. My wife had to deal with all the issues at home herself. She looked after our parents, bought us an apartment and decorated it. I could not do anything to help, so I would sometimes buy her something nice online, as a surprise to make her happy.

In December 2015, my daughter was born. Her birth created a deep bond that eased my lonely heart. I am now a husband and a father, but I do regret that I could not be by my wife's side when she needed me the most, and witness the birth of our daughter. Luckily, my wife never complained. In fact, she consoled me: "It's a bother flying all the way back and forth. You concentrate on your work."

Happiness

Return to Iceland

In 2013, the company began offshore delivery of services. The Global Technical Assistance Centre in Romania developed the capacity to maintain the CBS system remotely, so I was able to hand off my maintenance duties to them. I slotted naturally into the regional delivery team, and over the following period spent time working in Denmark, Sweden, the Czech Republic and Romania. All my experience stood me in good stead, and the projects went smoothly.

But, in November 2014, the CBS system and short message service (SMS) centre in Iceland needed to be upgraded. The pre-sales staff and the customer chose me to deliver this project because I knew the existing network well, and because the customer knew and trusted me. So, after a year away, I was back in Iceland once again.

Now that the project is coming to an end, I am about to leave this magical country that has brought me love, marriage and a family. Those days when I sat alone looking at the sky, the vistas of ice and snow, and the vast sea, are drawing to a close.

Iceland is such a tranquil and serene land. Nowhere else on this bustling planet can quite compare. An eight-year chapter of my life is about to end, and I will continue to work on other projects in the region. Iceland is in my blood, and will continue to inspire me. My experience there is also the most unforgettable and precious asset I have.

Mission to Medog

By Wang Wenzheng

Building the first mobile base station in Medog County, Tibet, was one of the most amazing experiences of my life. In 2004, I was assigned to build the satellite transmission station in Medog, which was the last county in China without any road access. This was part of Phase 5 of China Telecom's project to expand its network in Tibet. I was lucky enough to be the first Huawei employee to visit Medog, a part of the country so isolated that it was known as 'the lonely island on the plateau.' I was filled with pride and a sense of mission.

Mystery and isolation

Medog County is located in the southeast of Tibet, on the lower reaches of the Yarlung Tsangpo River. It covers an area of over 30,000 square kilometres. For Tibet, it is low: only 1,000 or so metres above sea level, on average. As such, it enjoys plentiful rainfall, and the natural environment is pristine. However, there were no roads connecting it to the outside world. In the 1970s, a rough road was built from Bomê County to Medog, spanning 144 kilometres, but it was destroyed in floods the very next year. The local government built roads every year, but they were constantly destroyed by landslides and mudslides, and by 2004 no complete road to the county had been built. Few people have visited the county, and all goods have to be carried in by porters. Rainfall, snow-capped mountains, virgin forests, mountain springs, water-falls, ethnic Monpa villages, porters, packhorses, shared sleeping mats at the way stations, 100-plus kilometres of footpath into and out of the county, landslides, avalanches … all of these and more contributed to the mystery of Medog County.

However, when I received the order to start work there, my excitement turned to anxiety and worry. It would take five days of hiking to reach Medog, and the thought of the landslides, mud-slides, leeches and poisonous snakes along the way almost frightened me off.

Suddenly, I remembered a famous quote by Nikolai Ostrovsky: "Man's dearest possession is life. It is given to him but once, and he must live it so as to feel no torturing regrets for wasted years, never know the burning shame of a mean and petty past." It's true. We only live once, and few people have the opportunity to visit a place like this. Now, I was lucky enough to have been sent on a mission to Medog. It would not only be a conquest of nature, but also a challenge to myself.

Still, it was a major responsibility to walk to Medog and set up the base station on my own. I counted my equipment very carefully indeed. Medog is hard to get to – in fact, it's unreachable during some seasons. If we were short of just one screw, we might not find another one for sale in the whole county.

On 10 June 2004, everything was ready. All the equipment was packed in waterproof bags. It would be carried by local porters. I carefully read all the documentation on building and maintaining a new base station. I spent a considerable amount of time going over the installation procedure and the special warnings. With the help of two senior engineers, Tan Daqi and Gao Changcheng, the initial commissioning of the base station and the satellite transmission equipment went quite smoothly. This gave me confidence for the work ahead.

Carrying our equipment to Medog County

Day 1: Departure
From Bayi to the way station at Pai

At 7 am on 11 June, I boarded a truck at the gate of China Telecom Nyingchi. The truck, loaded with our equipment, drove me out of the town of Bayi. My journey to Medog had started.

The team consisted of six members: team leader Tsering Tashi, deputy leader Lhapa Gyalpo, Cao, Wang, Zhang and me. Along the way we talked about setting up the network, and about all the strange stories that came out of Medog, so the time passed quickly.

It was 12 noon by the time we arrived at the Pai Township way station, four kilometres away from the centre of the town. Most deliveries to Medog passed through this station. There we found about 60–70 Monpa porters, who had come down from the mountains three or four days earlier to wait for us.

We wrote down their names and started to divide up the loads, and I was surprised that there were a number of women among the porters. The porters are a very special group of people. They are the lifeline of Medog. All supplies for the county – including food, medicines, steel, cement and corrugated iron for buildings – must be carried in by porters. They will haul anything up snow-capped mountains and through landslides and valleys. All they asked was how many packages and how many kilos.

It was 4 pm when we finished dividing the loads between all the porters. Dusk fell and the mists cleared for a moment, giving us a rare view of Mount Namjagbarwa, the world's 15th highest mountain, soaring 7,782 metres above sea level. The whole team felt excited to be off.

We held a gathering to launch the expedition in the evening. Everyone was drinking butter tea and singing. Our team leader, Tsering Tashi, sang 'Qomolangma,' China's most famous song about the mountain, which was just stunning. We emphasized that safety came first. Norbu, manager of the network department at China Telecom Nyingchi, also stressed several times that keeping everyone safe was our first priority, and completing the project came second. Norbu had trekked to Medog himself when he was young. He said he had been caught in a rainstorm lasting nine days, and all ten of his toenails had peeled off.

I had been so busy
looking at my feet that
I hadn't managed to
look at the amazing
Himalayan landscape.
And I hadn't even
managed to think.

Day 2: Crossing the Doshong La Pass

From the Pai way station to Lage (18 kilometres)

At 7 am on 12 June, two trucks left for the Doshong La pass. The road was bumpy and dangerous. The trucks weaved back and forth up the mountain switchbacks, sometimes having to make almost 180-degree turns. It took at least a three-point turn to get around those bends. The drivers hauled the steering wheel around and around. I felt extremely nervous. The trucks made great clanking and rattling noises, and as we got close to the pass, finally one of them gave a great crash. "That's torn it," the driver said. We stopped and went to have a look. One of the front wheels had fractured.

So, the hiking phase of our journey began ahead of schedule. The porters clambered out of the trucks, picked up their loads and started making for the Doshong La pass. We made for an impressive convoy, marching up that road. I looked at the porters, bent double under their heavy loads, and realized just how tough they were.

After about half an hour of walking, the road became steeper. The stream beside the road started to leap and bound down the mountain. The water was cold, as it was melt   water from the icy peaks. Soon, we couldn't tell where the road ended and the river started. As we climbed higher, we were forced to breathe harder, and our hearts were hammering. Our feet felt like lead. Close to the pass itself, a freezing wind started to howl, and the snow and fog set it. We started to feel dizzy and our ears ached.

When we reached 4,000 metres above sea level, the road was covered with snow and it became harder to walk. There was just a black trail in the snow, showing us where the path went. We had to follow this trail very carefully, because if we slipped on the steep slopes we could easily fall right off the mountain. It didn't bear thinking about. Luckily, after we climbed up the last steep section, the snowy road ahead became broader. Finally, we saw the pass ahead of us.

I had conquered the 4,200-metre-high Doshong La pass!

Through the snowy pass

The road down the other side of the mountain was also steep, and covered with stones. Also, it started to rain. We hobbled up and down over the stones, our feet permanently immersed in streams of icy water. They quickly went numb. But, as we descended, we got more oxygen, so at least our breathing gradually returned to normal. The stones were murder on our feet. Every step meant jolts of pain for our toes and knees. I started to understand why so many people lost their toenails on the path to Medog.

At about 2 pm, as we staggered through the rain and the pain, we saw smoke rising ahead. It was Lage, our camp for the first night. Lage is at an elevation of 3,200 metres. The camp was not much more than wood huts and plastic sheeting. Still, we made a beeline for those huts. Inside were the porters, who had arrived long before us and were now sitting by the fire, drinking tea. I peeled back a plastic sheet and discovered that the quilts on the big plank bed were damp, but at that moment I couldn't do anything but lie down. My whole body was aching. For someone who had spent too long in the city, without much exercise, this march was truly punishing. I was soaked through, and after lying down I started to feel the chill, so I quickly picked myself up and huddled close to the fire to dry my clothes. This became a routine for me over the next few days.

A camp along the way

I opened my bag and found that my notebook and packing list were half soaked, so I was worried our equipment might be wet, too. I asked our guide Shangga to check. Once we had confirmed that the packaging on our equipment was undamaged, I was finally able to relax.

In the evening, I wrapped myself in the damp sleeping bag, with its strong smell of smoke. Watching the rain patter and trickle down the plastic sheeting, we all quickly fell into a quiet mood and were soon fast sleep.

Day 3: Running the gauntlet of leeches
From Lage to Hanmi (28 kilometres)

At 7 am on 13 June, we left the Lage camp for Hanmi.

We spent that whole day walking through virgin forest. The road varied between water and mud, with stones and boulders everywhere. Some were the size of watermelons, some no bigger than a fist. We hopped from stone to stone during the early part of the walk, but soon we were exhausted, and we just waded through the water and silt.

On that day, I came to understand why people say, "The road to Medog is harder than you could have ever imagined."

We arrived at Daai Hollow after two hours. We ate some instant noodles and rubbed our feet with alcohol. Our guide Shangga said, "There will be leeches on our way ahead." We were very nervous, as we had never seen leeches before. We cinched our trouser legs tight and put on gloves, despite the hot weather.

About an hour later, we saw our first leech during a rest stop in a clearing. It was a yellow and black mollusc. Its suckers were stuck firmly to a leaf, and its head stuck out, waiting for prey to pass.

We were all curious and crowded round to take pictures. When I returned to the path and rolled up my sleeve to look at my watch, I was astonished to see a big yellow and black leech stuck on my left arm. It was wriggling and getting bigger and bigger, and blood was already running down my wrist. "A leech has got me!" I yelled. It took a moment for everyone to realize what I was saying, but when I yelled again, they came running over.

Shangga was about to take the leech off, but Zhang stopped him. "Wait! Let me take a picture first."

I had to stand there in pain for several more seconds for his precious picture. I didn't know whether to laugh or cry at that moment. Once Zhang was done, Shangga quickly dispatched the leech with salt.

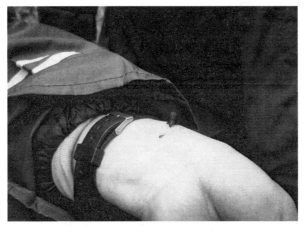

Bitten by a leech

There were more and more leeches as we continued. They were everywhere on the grass and leaves beside the road. After a few minutes' walking, we would find more than a dozen on our shoes and trousers. As we had leggings and rain-proof pants, the leeches couldn't bite our legs. But they crawled upwards, and some even got close to our necks. Disgusting creatures! Everyone became hyper-sensitive. Whenever we felt the slightest itch, we would immediately stop to check for leeches. But you could not stay in a state of extreme tension forever. After a while, we calmed down. Later on, whenever I spotted a leech on me, I'd just grab it, roll it up and flick it away.

The road seemed endless and we pushed ourselves to go faster because of the leeches. At 5 pm, we finally arrived at the Hanmi camp and saw a row of wooden barracks in the trees. We would spend the night there. The grass and the trees around the camp were full of leeches. It was quite a sight to see the six of us sitting in a row outside the door of our hut, taking off our shoes, pants and coats to kill all leeches with cigarettes and salt. I went over my clothes several times, found more than 20 leeches, and killed them all before I thought it was safe to go inside. I was sharing a room with Cao. The black quilts smelled like they had gone mouldy. We sat on the bed, still checking for more leeches. Although the rain was not heavy, our clothes had become totally drenched with sweat, because our raincoats were not breathable. The wet clothes made us extremely cold, so we sat close to the fire to get warmer. After a simple supper, I checked the bed and sleeping bag once again and rubbed my painful legs with alcohol. Cao was close to 40 years old, and he was exhausted. As we lay there, waiting to sleep, he said, "This isn't a job. This is a suicide mission!" He made me laugh. In a way, it had not been an exciting day, as I had been so busy looking at my feet that I hadn't managed to look at the amazing Himalayan landscape. And I hadn't even managed to think.

Day 4: Through the virgin forest
From Hanmi to Bipung (36 kilometres)

We had been lucky with the weather. Each day, the rain lasted the whole night, but it stopped early in the morning. Soon after 7 am, the six of us set off along the track, which was muddy after last night's rain. About three hours later, we reached the section known as 'tiger's mouth.' The path here used to be very dangerous. It passed through a hollow in the side of a cliff (the tiger's mouth), and it was easy to slip and fall. But it was no longer as bad as it used to be: the path was now one-metre wide, making it somewhat safer. But the streams running down the mountain sprayed onto the path like little waterfalls, drenching us from head to toe. Below us, they flowed deep into the chasm. We cautiously lined up and walked slowly along the path, each keeping a safe distance from the other.

On the other side of the tiger's mouth, we were wet through with spray and sweat. We kept on trudging through the untouched Tibetan forests. The path weaved up and down hills and valleys, and we had to cross several steel-cable suspension bridges. We had put salt in our shoes to deter leeches, but the mud seeped in and turned it to a salty stew in there. As I had several blisters and injuries on my feet, this was exceedingly painful! My knees were also registering a dull protest, and by the afternoon the pain in my calves meant that I could barely pick up my feet.

We descended from 4,200 metres to around 1,000 metres, and passed from the alpine belt into subtropical rainforest. The weather was heavy and hot. Our canteens were swiftly emptying, and it seemed that every mouthful of water we drank went back to the earth in the form of sweat. We were now in a subtropical paradise, with banana trees all around us. This is the only part of Tibet where bananas grow. But it was not the right season, so our mouths watered for nothing.

The sun was scorching and the temperature was rising. My raincoat was stifling, so it felt like I was walking in my own portable sauna. But, I didn't dare to take the coat off in case of leeches. So I struggled on, with sweat coursing down my back. The road seemed to go on forever. Our canteens were now completely dry, and we were approaching a state of total exhaustion. My lips had cracked.

Only willpower kept me moving on along that seemingly endless path. When we finally spotted the Liberation Bridge, the last landmark on the way to Bipung, I nearly burst into tears. I didn't know whether it was from excitement or pain.

At 8:30 pm, we finally reached Bipung, our stop for the fourth day. We had trudged for 13 hours through the forest. We checked ourselves for leeches, and then everyone sat, exhausted, on the wooden steps of the Bipung municipal hostel. I used some of the Erguotou spirit I had brought to disinfect my scratches and blisters. My feet had been soaking in salty, muddy water for nearly eight hours. They were red and inflamed and extremely painful.

Day 5: The last stop
From Bipung to Medog (33 kilometres)
I had been in pain the whole night. In the morning, when I looked at my feet, I saw that some of the wounds were oozing pus, and some had opened right up. I needed a day to recover. To make sure that I would not fall behind, Tashi and Lhapa rented a mule from a neighbouring village. On the fifth day, we were basically trekking along the flat banks of the Yarlung Tsangpo River, and that made mule-riding possible. Lucky me! That said, I was rather embarrassed when I saw that Cao, who was a lot older than me, still had to walk.

Despite the rain the previous night, the weather cleared nicely in the morning. The sun shone as bright as if it meant to make up for all the sombreness of the past few days. Walking along the muddy path, the feet of my colleagues were soon covered with mud and started to weigh a ton. "There's a good three pounds of mud on there," Cao said. Riding on the mule, I saw my colleagues trudging down the road under the fierce sun. Though it didn't seem much, I helped by carrying canteens for them.

Unforgettable trip to Medog

At 7:30 pm, we finally climbed the last, long mountain slope. The beautiful Medog was bathed in the rays of the setting sun. This was the town we had been dreaming of! The six of us hugged each other, full of emotion, and then we went crazy, throwing our hats in the air, waving our walking sticks and screaming proudly, "Medog, here we are!"

Tsundue, head of the Medog telecommunications bureau, had prepared a feast for us. After so much pain on the long trek, we enjoyed the sweet taste of victory. It was the most delicious meal of my life.

Mobile Medog

The residents were very excited about the prospect of having mobile phone coverage for the first time. Medog only had four satellite lines to the outside world, and they were mostly reserved for incoming calls only. While we were still installing the equipment, many villagers rushed to buy mobile phones. I keenly felt the weight of their expectations. The head of Medog County came to the equipment room several times to see how we were progressing. "When will we be connected?" he asked.

Installing antennas

Due to the rain and the humidity, my first job was to check whether the equipment had gotten wet. None of the packages had leaked, but some of the boards were damp. I aired them for half a day and spent two hours drying them with a hairdryer before I thought it was safe to connect them. After two days, we finally had everything installed. We powered the system up and made all the necessary commissioning. By this time, more than 170 mobile numbers had been allocated. The phones we had brought in soon sold out, so the Nyingchi telecommunications bureau had hired porters to bring in more phones.

This was the first time I had ever built a new network. I didn't have any experience doing this kind of work. And it was the first time Huawei had ever installed a mini station for satellite transmission. This meant that the commissioning process was difficult. There wasn't any way to easily get help, so I had to work it out myself. I worked through the night, from 10 pm on 18 June to 5:20 am on 19 June, first with a satellite engineer, to get the satellite link working. Then I upgraded the boards at my end, and we switched to the satellite link. With a little help from my colleague in Lhasa, suddenly the Medog base station went live.

I stood outside the base station, and made Medog's first mobile call to the outside world. It was an exciting moment for me! I had trekked here, representing Huawei, to this 'lonely island,' and I had done something real for the people of this tough little town. And, despite not being with the company for very long, I had built and booted up a whole new network from scratch. I felt a lot of pride in my accomplishment, and I was too excited to sleep that night.

Inside the Huawei base station

Blaze your own trail

After the job was done, we set out on the return journey. Having suffered the painful trek from Pai to Medog, no one wanted to go back via that road. We decided to take a different path, via Bomê County. That way we would get to see the whole county, we thought. We chose to travel through a place called 80K, which is 80 kilometres from Bomê County and would lead us out of Medog. But it would likely be another challenge. The path would lead us over complex terrain, with frequent landslides and mudslides, so it was more dangerous than the route via Pai. Still, the weather was good, so we voted and persuaded Norbu to take on the 80-kilometre challenge. The weather helped us a lot on the way back. Most of the time, it rained at night and the sun came out in the day. Maybe it was a reward for our efforts on behalf of the people of Medog.

Network connected, on the way home

After trekking for four straight days, covering 144 kilometres through a landslide danger zone, we arrived in Bomê County. Lying on my hotel bed, I thought about our eight days trudging through the virgin forest on the way to and back from Medog, and our eight nights in primitive campsites. I couldn't sleep at the thought of those porters, each of whom carried nearly 50 kilograms of loads on their back over that same route. They live in such a tough and dangerous environment. Life is so fragile and so precious. Many people have lost their lives on the road to Medog, in landslides or avalanches. We live blessed lives compared to them. We have every reason to work hard and be nice to our families and friends. We must cherish and make the most of every minute of our lives.

Back in Lhasa, I still couldn't stop visualizing our trek to Medog whenever I closed my eyes. It was a road with no end. It was a road that only bull-headed stubbornness could get us through. The so-called 'road' to Medog was no road at all. It was only a route people chose to walk. It is a rare opportunity to choose our own path, no matter what danger or difficulties that may entail. Taking the road less travelled will reward you with extraordinary experiences.

Sometimes I think we need a little excitement to enrich our lives. The trek to Medog did not lead to epic discoveries, like Columbus finding America. However, it gave me a new perspective on how people can live in harsh environments, with their backs heavy but unbowed.

Sometimes I think that if you pass through landslide danger zones from time to time, isn't that a way to remind yourself to value the path you have taken? You should appreciate what you have, and work hard for what you don't have. There will be flowers in full blossom along the way, and there will be fallen flowers, too. There will be ups and downs as we march forward. As long as we keep moving forward, not fearing the hardships down the road, we will get through it. On the long and hard journey of life, I believe I have the guts to face up to the many difficulties life might throw at me.

I've been thinking that if I have the chance to go to Medog a second time, I would be happy to take it. The path to Medog has etched a deep groove in my heart, a life experience I'll never forget.

At the Epicentre

By Matsumoto Yasufumi

It was January 2006. I left a career in NEC and Nokia, two big names in the communications industry, and joined Huawei, an unproven minnow back then. Everybody thought I was out of my mind.

Huawei had just established a subsidiary in Japan. Its rented offices, covering an area of more than 1,000 square metres, were in Tokyo's most expensive business district, Ōtemachi. Despite this extravagance, the company was totally unknown to Japanese people. They had no idea where Huawei came from or what the company did. Even people from the communications industry knew little about it and couldn't pronounce the name 'Huawei' properly.

Many people kept asking why I had chosen to come to Huawei. The answer was actually simple: I just thought it would be fun to go back to square one. If we failed, the company would fold. It seemed like a great opportunity for me personally to test how good I really was. Why not go for it?

Yan Lida, who was General Manager of the Japan Office back then, says, "Every person who joined Huawei at that point was risking a lot. And we fought many tough battles together. I'm so lucky to have been a member of this team."

Today, I am the longest-serving Japanese person in the company. I'm glad I made that choice 10 years ago.

Going all out for success with our customer

We were very lucky to find ourselves presented with a once-in-a-lifetime opportunity. The Japanese government issued three mobile licenses to increase competition in the market. A new player, Operator E, had obtained one license and was looking for an ambitious, energetic partner. Huawei caught their eye.

Though Huawei seemed a perfect match, Operator E was still rather doubtful about working with a newcomer to the Japanese market. They wondered whether Huawei's quality was good enough. They were putting their company's life in our hands, after all. But they had no idea how committed we were to focusing our energy on them. We had decided to do whatever it took to help them succeed.

One of the co-founders of Operator E is from Hong Kong. He speaks very good English, which made his exchange with Yan Lida quite productive. One weekend, he drove Yan to a restaurant where Yan explained to him the latest developments in the wireless market, the key challenges facing new mobile operators, and the solutions that Huawei could offer. Yan recommended Huawei's distributed base stations. Impressed by what Yan said, he banged on the table, and yelled with excitement, "This is exactly what we've been looking for!"

Then we took people from Operator E to visit Huawei headquarters and our demo sites. After intense negotiations and some six months of back-and-forth on the contract, we finally inked a deal with Operator E in June 2006. And that was the time when Huawei truly became a player in the Japanese market.

It was only half a year since I had joined the company, and already I had a sweet taste of victory. It was extremely exciting! I told myself I would do this job to the very best of my ability to help our customer succeed. After all, Operator E was the only customer we had in the Japanese market at that time. Over the next period, I slept in the office three or four days a week. Sometimes there was not even time to grab lunch. I once stayed awake for three days straight. Not a single minute's sleep for two nights! Everybody was working really hard, and enjoying it.

People often say that Japanese people value teamwork, while Chinese people prefer the heroic individual. After spending some time with Chinese colleagues, I saw that this was not true. My Huawei colleagues were all great team players. Everyone worked hard toward the same goal. Another quality that I admire in my Chinese colleagues is that when they make mistakes, they turn inward and do self-reflection, which is rarely seen in other companies.

Unlike companies that ran in the face of danger, I was now sure that Huawei was a company with a conscience: a responsible company that deserves my life-long dedication.

To evacuate or to stay?

What makes me even prouder of the company is how it reacted in the face of natural disasters.

At 2 pm JST on 11 March 2011, a magnitude-9.0 earthquake rocked the northeast coast of Japan, followed by a tsunami. We felt a small jolt in the middle of a meeting in Atami, 100 kilometres outside Tokyo. Everybody knew about earthquakes, so we remained calm until we saw on television what was going on. At 3:25 pm, the tsunami hit the coast near Rikuzentakata. It swept through the city centre at 3:26 pm. At 3:43 pm, all we could see from the screen was the rooftop of the four-storey city hall. In an instant, an entire city was submerged under the ocean. I had seen many earthquakes, but this time it was much more violent than ever before, and was worse than I could imagine.

I rushed home from Atami, hopping from one bus to another to get there as fast as I could. As I got close, I saw all the fallen houses. Obviously, this place had been seriously hit. I charged in through my front door, but no one was there. My heart nearly stopped. What was going on? Where had they all gone? I quickly called my wife. On the other end of the phone was a commotion, but my wife said they were just fetching water from water dispensers, because the electricity and water supplies had both been cut off. Finally, my heart started beating again.

It was not long before explosions began at the Fukushima Daiichi Nuclear Power Plant, causing radioactive leaks. Radioactive materials were blown by the wind, and we began to hear warnings from Tokyo of dangerous radiation levels. The nuclear meltdown was an unmitigated disaster, casting a pall over everyone's heart. Our peers quickly began evacuating staff and their families to Osaka, with some even chartering planes to Hong Kong. As a result, some of us started to panic.

To evacuate or to stay? To be honest, the Japanese staff had nowhere to go. We belong here. Japan is our home. The Huawei Japan management team stayed, too. They were in the office every day, following the latest developments and keeping everyone updated. To keep the team feeling confident, Yan Lida stayed in Tokyo throughout the entire crisis. His family was also in Tokyo for much of that time.

I remember clearly the night of 15 March, when I read a long letter from Yan. He wrote it in English, addressed to all employees of Huawei Japan, and it was heartfelt. He explained to us how management saw the situation and their intentions in the wake of the earthquake. He said Huawei should step up to its responsibility as a corporate citizen, and should stay with our customers. He also told us that the risks were controllable, and that the decision to stay was not a rash one. In addition, the company had developed a contingency plan to make sure everyone, both Chinese and Japanese, could be evacuated in the case of emergency. We were very moved. One of my Japanese colleagues immediately wrote back to him: "I am bowing to you in respect!"

Then Huawei's Chairwoman, Madam Sun Yafang, came. She addressed all the staff in an open area in front of the office building. She said the company had sent her to check on whether we were alright, and to offer her support. She told us to persevere and take care of ourselves. Afterwards, she went to see the engineers who could not come because they were running tests in the lab. Our customer was stunned. "Your chairwoman came to visit in person, while other vendors are scrambling to get out of here?" When the customer's senior management found out about the visit, they were also shocked, saying: "That is a truly heroic story!"

Huawei's CFO, Meng Wanzhou, also quickly arrived at the Japan Office. When she flew from Hong Kong to Japan, she was one of only two passengers on the flight. The other passenger on her flight, a Japanese person, even asked whether she had taken the wrong flight. After arriving in Japan, Ms Meng worked with us to review the execution of our contingency plan, and discussed post-disaster work arrangements, including our plans to repair customer networks.

To assuage some of our worries, the company later sent our families and nonessential personnel to Osaka, including local staff. But, not one of the 40 or so key project members left.

During that period, no one was fighting alone. Everyone worked together, Chinese and local staff, as a tight-knit unit. Wherever there was a problem or danger, there was always a helping hand. I already knew that Huawei was a great company from China, but after this whole thing I realized it was much more than this. Unlike companies that ran in the face of danger, I was now sure that Huawei was a company with a conscience: a responsible company that deserves my life-long dedication.

"You can do it! I just know."

What concerned us most was our customer's network. Power outages and collapsing buildings had knocked out some of Operator E's base stations in quake-hit areas. We reached out to Operator E at the earliest time possible, asking how we could help. For safety reasons, they wanted to restore their network on their own. Nevertheless, the engineers and contractors whom we had sent to support the reconstruction did not leave. They chose to stay there, offering support whenever necessary. In the meantime, the nuclear leak got worse. The Japanese government declared a quarantine area, to which access was strictly controlled. We did what we could, delivering power supplies and power generators from outside the danger zone.

As power and transportation were gradually restored, 13 non-functional base stations were returned to service. In late March, Operator E approached us, asking whether we could provide mobile base stations and satellite transmission solutions to help with the issues they were unable to resolve on their own.

All they had to do was ask. We were 100% ready to help. Without any delay, our quake zone engineers went to the sites. As they checked out the sites, they stayed in real-time communication with those back at the office so we could quickly find solutions to the problems. Some base stations were soon restored. However, there were a few knotty problems too difficult for the onsite engineers to resolve. We needed experts.

To support our customer's request for mobile base stations, to provide communications services for people displaced by the disaster, management decided to send an elite team out to help. The team comprised one expert from China and three of our Japanese employees. I was one of them.

Before I left for the assignment, I told my wife, "I'm going to help restore communications in the quake zone." She was shocked, but quickly composed herself. "I suppose that's necessary, isn't it?" I knew she must be very upset deep down inside. And she should be. That assignment entailed danger for sure. But she herself was working at NEC. She knew that specialist support would be needed to get the communications networks functioning again. At these critical moments, no one but us could get the job done. So, no matter how conflicted and worried she was, she tried to remain calm and told me to take extra care of myself. She said encouragingly, "You can do it! I just know."

I was very grateful for her understanding and support. She knew it was our responsibility to do it, and that gave me great courage and strength.

Consolation in a desert

Before leaving, we prepared everything we would need to deploy mobile base stations in densely populated quake-hit areas: a careful plan, the locations of the 40 base stations that need repairing, and four emergency communications vehicles.

At dusk on 5 April, we left Tokyo for Sendai. We were feeling calm. All we were thinking about was how we could get there as quickly as possible to restore services for the many people affected by the disaster. On the way, we passed through Fukushima, only 50 or 60 kilometres away from the nuclear power station. Our radiation detector started to beep, indicating that the radiation level was 20 times higher than in Tokyo. We set the detector to vibrate mode and continued driving.

The next day, we arrived at the worst-hit place, Rikuzentakata. It had been devastated by both the earthquake and the tsunami. When we turned off the highway, we saw farmland and houses, intact and peaceful. It was as if there had been no disaster. But when we drove about one kilometre further on, suddenly all the houses were gone. There was nothing left but a heap of rubble and a wilderness of fallen houses and destroyed cars, the broken remains of a town swallowed by the tsunami. Houses had collapsed on mobile towers, and everything was twisted out of shape. An acrid smell hung in the air, spreading a mood dismal beyond words. How could a town just vanish overnight?

Devastation in Rikuzentakata

All the bridges, railways and highways were damaged. The only passage to the disaster scene was a single temporary road sorted out by the Self-Defense Forces. We elbowed our way along the congested road to a base station high on a platform in the hills. The freezing wind penetrated my face, my neck and my hair like needles. The bird's eye view from the platform captured a lifeless town: a grim desert of fallen houses, many reduced to just a few steel reinforcing rods sticking out of the mud. What was the point of restoring these base stations, I wondered. No one is going to use them. No one is ever coming here again!

The cold wind eventually calmed me down. I collected myself. Many people affected by the disaster were waiting for communications capabilities, to call for help and comfort. There was no time for grief.

The whole area was seriously damaged and we didn't have any equipment. It occurred to me that we could mount our antennas on mobile cranes. The antenna could point in the direction of the relief shelter, and connect to our data centres via satellite. On 7 April, we built a new mobile base station in Ofunato. It took just half a day to install and commission our equipment, add a satellite receiver and install the antenna. At dusk, it started working. It didn't look like much, but that base station enabled the people affected by the disaster there to make phone calls!

The DIY base station

It was past 10 pm when we got back to the hotel. The four of us went to bed at about 11 o'clock, because we still needed to commission two more base stations the next day. But soon we were awakened by violent up-and-down jolts and the earthquake alarm on our mobile phones. The power was off, and emergency lamps were on. The high-frequency up-and-down motion, along with the slamming of windows and doors, lasted for one or two minutes. I felt like this was stronger than the quake that happened on 11 March, but there was nothing I could do except wait it out. Luckily, it soon stopped and power was restored. We learned from the news that this quake had been a 6.0, and the epicentre was nearby. We calmed ourselves down, and then called the Tokyo office to let them know we were safe before going back to sleep.

Within a week, we brought 40 base stations back online for our customer, and set up several temporary ones. We had brought radiation detectors with us, but no one was really thinking about the radiation at that point. We just wanted to help all those in need as soon as possible. We wanted to help them at least make a phone call to their loved ones to say hello, to hear a friendly voice for some consolation. Then, everything we were doing would be worthwhile.

On 27 April, we went back a second time to check that all the temporary base stations were functioning properly. Our local engineers never left the disaster zone until all base stations were restored.

After the earthquake, people asked me, "What compensation did your employer give you for going into the most dangerous places?" Truth be told, I didn't get any money at all, but we did receive a Golden Medal Award. As a Japanese member of the Huawei team, I felt it was my responsibility to do my bit during that critical period, and I was proud to contribute.

A few months ago, a Japanese magazine interviewed me and I retold this story of five years ago. Our actions proved how much Huawei cares about and is committed to its customers. I am just happy to say that I worked on the front lines of disaster relief.

Five-Star Payment Craftsman:
14 Years Without a Single Error

By Big Sister Ma

In 1999, I earned my master's degree and joined Huawei as a payment accountant in the finance team.

When I first started as the new girl in the office, I felt so young. Now, nearly 20 years later, I am a mentor and our fresh-faced newbies all call me 'Big Sister.' I started my career as a payment accountant, but today I am a final approver of payments. Over two decades, I have handled hundreds of transactions and claims each day, ranging in value from a few yuan to hundreds of millions of yuan. My records show that I have processed 1.05 million payments, and it has now been 14 years since I made my last error during processing.

In 2019, I was honoured to be voted the only 'Five-Star Payment Craftsman' during the fourth round of payment craftsmen selection, organized by the finance team. This is the highest level of commendation that anyone in my line of work can receive, and was the biggest honour I've ever been awarded.

People often ask me how I have managed to go so long without making any errors. After all, no one is perfect. But the truth is, my 14-year streak started with two huge errors.

The two errors that led to a perfect 14-year run

My first job with Huawei was as a cashier, which is currently known as a payment accountant. As I was one of the few employees in my department with a master's degree, I was both ambitious and confident. I wasn't pleased about being put in this lower-level position. At the time, I thought to myself: this job is beneath me. However, I made two critical errors within just one month. It was a real blow to my confidence.

These two errors had a significant impact on my career, and even today, after so long, I can still remember every detail of what happened.

We were dealing with two suppliers with very similar names – just one or two letters different. When I was checking the documents, I didn't notice the difference, and combined the two payments to the two companies into one. It was a sum of about US$1,000.

A few days later, I was making a payment to another supplier. I should have deducted an advance payment we had already made, but I didn't, instead making the full payment, this time for about US$2,000.

When the department did its monthly review of bank statements, these two critical errors were detected. When my department head sat me down and very seriously explained them to me, I was stunned. But, she did not blame me. Instead, she patiently reviewed what had happened to identify the cause of my mistakes before finally asking a question that gave me pause. "Have you ever asked yourself whether you actually like this job?"

That single question both shook me and brought me clarity. I realized that all of this had been caused by my attitude: I was overconfident and under-skilled, and I had not given my work the attention it deserved. I was trying to dash through my tasks as quickly as I could. I had not seen the job for what it was: the first step on a long road. As a result, I had made some easily avoidable mistakes. I was very upset with myself, "I can't even get this right! What am I thinking? I have to get the basics right first!" But, there was no way I would have been satisfied leaving the job on such a sour note. To this day, I am grateful for how my department head handled the situation. She gave me another chance, and together we contacted the suppliers to correct the errors.

From that day on, I have lived by a new mantra: if you can't do the little things right, it will be impossible to do the big things right.

No matter how urgent a request is, or how familiar I am with a payment procedure and the related checkpoints, I circle and double check all key information on every payment voucher I issue. After I fill in the documents, I make sure to check each item, one by one. I remind myself that this is not just arithmetic homework. Money matters! So, I force myself to stay focused and cool-headed: more speed, less haste. I carefully review each and every checkpoint to make sure everything is done right the first time. I don't want to lock the stable door after the horse has bolted. To me, the secret to my zero-error run, which has involved tens of thousands of payments, is simple: as long as I am careful, focused and patient, I can ensure that each payment is accurate and on schedule.

Whenever I have time, I sort out all the documents needed for payment: contracts, customs declaration forms, receipt statements, foreign exchange applications, etc. That way, I don't get flustered when the payments start rolling in.

I spent six years working as a payment accountant, churning through payment data day-in and day-out. Over those six years, I never once made an error. In 2006, I was assigned to the Argentina Shared Services Centre as a cashier, after which I was moved into payroll and then worked as a chief accountant. In 2011, my manager asked whether I wanted to serve as a bank account signatory, performing the final checks before money leaves the company.

Huawei has a business presence in over 100 countries and regions. Every day, the company makes tens of thousands of payments, adding up to hundreds of millions of US dollars. Everything the company buys has to be signed off by a bank account signatory, whether it's a new potted plant for a meeting room, paper clips for an office, or a million-dollar payment to a component supplier.

I knew better than most that this job would not allow for mistakes. Any mistake I made could cause the company's cash to go bowling out the door, so the responsibility was a heavy one. I had to ask myself, was I truly ready for this responsibility?

Over the previous five years in particular, I had made attempts to assume managerial positions. However, I always found that I was more adept at dealing with data. My many years serving as a payment accountant had also made me particularly rigorous and meticulous at work. I was confident that I would make a good bank account signatory, and, if the company was willing to put its trust in me, then I was determined to become the best!

Applying over 40 seals, 3,000 times per day

One of the key responsibilities of a bank account signatory is to endorse payments with company seals. Company seals have great power. They are like the signatures of ancient commanders, capable of sending thousands of soldiers marching back and forth. The slightest error when using company seals can lead to incalculable losses.

The first time I opened the two boxes I had been given, and was faced with the more than 40 different company seals used for financial documents, I almost fainted. I looked down upon dozens of seals of different colours, materials and shapes. There was horn, bronze, red rubber and black ink. Some were self-inking and others used photosensitive ink. Some were round, some oval, and others square. Some had covers, some did not. Shenzhen used round seals made of horn, while Chengdu had adopted square, self-inking ones. I needed to memorize the position and name of each seal within the boxes, so that I could quickly find what I needed while processing around 1,000 payment documents every day.

How on earth was I going to use them? I had absolutely no idea. These seals had previously been looked after by multiple finance managers, but after I became the bank account signatory, they handed all of them over to me. I became the sole manager of the seals; no one else knew how they were supposed to be used. There was no one to teach me, so I had to rely on myself. I searched online for answers, and found that the use of seals was not a simple proposition. Different seals require different types of ink: traditional inkpads, photosensitive ink, special ink for self-inking stamps, you name it. Each kind of stamp needs to be inked in a different way. This may be by using an inkpad, refilling from the top, or turning the stamp upside down. There were stern warnings online: don't mix your inks or you might destroy the seals!

After a few days' research, I took some scrap paper and tried them all out. They should have been easy to use by that point. However, when I tried to use them, I found it was hard to create an adequate stamp. If you didn't get it just right, the image would be smeared or too light. Sometimes, the seal would slip on the desk. But, if I put a pad under the paper, the surface would be too soft, distorting the impression. I spent a whole night on it, trying all possible positions: I sat, I stood, I bent. I tried to apply the seal with my left hand, right hand, and then both hands. I put a magazine and a calendar under the paper. Finally, I found the perfect method: putting the document to be endorsed on a mouse pad, and then applying the seal. After over a week's practice, I had figured out the best standard procedure for myself: hold the seal in your right hand; line it up; press down with the left hand on the right hand; and silently count to three.

During the course of my work, I also discovered that each document has its own rules for sealing, so there was a lot to learn. For example, there are six major things you want to avoid when endorsing bank acceptance bills: don't let the stamp spill over any lines on the bill; don't cover over other seals or signatures; don't tilt the seal; don't blur the seal; don't use the wrong seal; and don't forget to stamp across the perforations. When I had finally internalized all of these rules, I was finally able to use my standardized procedure to produce perfect impressions.

I started to love the beautiful patterns of a well-applied stamp. To me, they were more refreshing than a sunset in the mountains, the breeze on a lake, or birdsong in a wood. It's no exaggeration to say that when I wield my stamps, my mind's eye sees the smiles of people worldwide as they use their phones.

Using the company seals is a technical skill that also requires physical strength. More than that, though, the seals test both your willpower and speed. Before host-to-host payment was widely deployed to directly connect Huawei with its banks, I would have to apply the seals 2,000–3,000 times a day during peak periods. If I worked eight hours a day, I would have to, conservatively, process 2,000 endorsements each day. That is the equivalent of applying one seal every 15 seconds.

Faced with a huge stack of documents, I developed a procedure that I still follow today. I start by taking a deep breath. Then, I begin sorting the documents by importance and urgency. I first handle confirmations for Huawei's bank accounts submitted by the sales team. Then, I start on the fund management documents, where banks set clear deadlines, such as for transfers between accounts and treasury deal documents. Following that, I work on regular payments. I leave bank acceptance bills until the very last, because they have the strictest requirements and there are always lots of them. Every time I endorse a document, I double-check it to make certain there are no errors. After repeating this stamping procedure for some time, it was burned into my muscle memory.

During some busy periods, I would work from morning until night. When I finally got home for dinner, at eight or nine in the evening, my hands were often so worn out that I could barely feed myself. In those moments, I would always plan to start a regimen of regular push-ups to improve my strength ... but somehow that never happened!

Looking at the bigger picture saved US$3 million

Many people wonder how I have avoided making a single mistake for 14 years straight. Is it because I'm just a stickler for detail?

In truth, it's got nothing to do with my personal character. I am actually a very laid back kind of person. With my job, though, I must be strict with myself. During approval, I have to know whether a transaction will be profitable or generate losses; whether it has been approved and booked in compliance with company processes; and whether I, as a bank account signatory, have the authority to sign off on documents relating to this type of transaction. I need to check all of these things, one by one, as there is no room for error. Protecting Huawei's money requires business acumen, strict compliance with procedures and high quality output.

Business acumen is built upon a solid understanding of accounting basics. That means I have to be very familiar with every accounting module, assess the accuracy of data from different business documents based on real accounting data, and stick firmly to basic principles. I still remember that in 2016, one business department needed me to sign off on an application for some awards. Their department head had approved the use of seals in the e-flow, but the data source for the sales figures of one of the products was missing. I kept digging until I got to the bottom of it – the sales volume was double the actual figure. So, I rejected this request. After that, I refined the protocol for using financial seals, and business departments must now have their financial data approved by their financial controller if they need something sealed.

Over the years, I have identified transaction issues worth over US$479 million. I've also rejected several unreasonable sealing requests and requests containing incorrect data.

The next thing I have to do every day is ensure strict compliance with procedures. I like to learn new things, so I always take the time to learn the ins and outs of an entire process. When working on documents, I often spend time checking things that others might think are completely pointless, and I never take things at face value. Deep-diving into documents can help me spot problems more quickly. For example, what bank is a payee using? Usually, you would assume that it is the bank named in our accounting system. But, assumptions are the root of many errors. One Huawei employee had the People's Bank of China – China's central bank – as his payroll account bank in our accounting system. Obviously, that's not possible!

I like to check things, even if they are (strictly speaking) not my responsibility. In theory, as long as I can see that the process has been followed, then I should sign off on a payment. But, as I am the final check for payments, I impose stricter requirements based on my experience and business acumen. As far as I'm concerned, responsibilities cannot be confined to a specific role. So, in addition to checking process compliance, I check whether payments are normal and reasonable, just to make sure we're not about to complacently step on a landmine.

One day in 2013, a subsidiary informed me that it needed to pay a large amount of money to a supplier. The subsidiary said that it was an urgent request, as the local bank was going to close soon. All of the approval documentation was in order, but I knew all the subsidiaries that normally made large supplier payments, and this one was not on that list. So, I went back and checked the whole process, looking at the original documents. I had a feeling that something was wrong. It turned out that the invoice being paid was issued two years ago. The payment was close to US$3 million. In fact, the supplier and Huawei were still in the process of settling a dispute, so the payment had to be frozen.

Checking for problems is simple enough, but the instinct that allows me to spot these problems has developed from more than a decade of experience. Without it, I would never have achieved my long error-free run.

I think we must remain as committed to our jobs as we were on the first day. Then, in years to come, we can hold our heads up and say that we have done our part for this company, and for society as a whole.

Working together to create synergy

I don't take all the credit for my perfect run. It would have been impossible without the wisdom of the whole payment team and the company's financial transformation.

As a long-time employee, I have witnessed the transformation Huawei Finance has undergone over the past 20 years. In 1999, the payment centre had a dozen employees, who mainly used an ERP system and manual processing of financial documents to serve company-level functions. At the end of each month and year, we were overwhelmed by documentation. We would have four or five boxes filled with stacks of documents half a metre high. I often felt like I was drowning in a sea of documents. However, this was my work. My impatience was gradually tempered, and I eventually learned to keep calm despite the pressure.

The finance team has been constantly transforming, establishing new standards and unified processes and moving closer to automation – putting effective systems in place to support these processes. We also employ the best tools and technologies we can find to simplify processes and guarantee data accuracy. Many 'advanced weapons' are used in our day-to-day payment activities.

Before 2007, each payment document had to be filled out manually by individual employees, signed off in pen by the bank account signatory, and sent to banks by other designated employees. This meant that each employee in the payment team could only process around 20 transactions per day.

In 2008, the company started using e-banking payments, which allowed us to upload payment instructions in batches. This meant that when a bank account signatory gave the green light for an e-bank payment, the related instructions could go straight to the banks. At this stage, each of us could process about 200 transactions per day.

In 2012, the company's ERP system allowed payment instructions to be sent to banks directly. This simplification in processes increased per capita efficiency to 5,000 transactions per day.

Finally, in 2016, we launched a payment strategy centre. Different payment rules have now been directly embedded in the system. Payment security is essentially guaranteed through system operations and manual checks. In 2013, the payment error rate was 0.00651%. In 2018, not a single payment process error was made over the course of the whole year.

As time passes, business changes. Not only do we now face higher workloads, we also have to meet higher requirements. Operational procedures, deadlines and accounting rules vary from bank to bank. Some banking platforms use languages other than English and Chinese. In such cases, we have to translate their webpages and ensure that all of our data is correct. This increases risk, meaning we have to be even more vigilant. We can never be too careful in our work.

In the past, correct payments were confirmed by checking payer and payee information. Today, we must achieve not only correct payments, but also successful payments. That means we have to check the accuracy of each and every piece of information about a transaction, including the handling fees, payment purpose and payee addresses. What's more, some countries or regions require additional information to complete a successful transaction, and all of these fields must be 100% correct.

Fortunately, we have over 100 colleagues in the Global Payment Centre. We work hard together, have clear responsibilities and roles, and share the same goals. We start each day by checking pending payment data in the system and methodically checking pending and abnormal data in our e-banking system. No matter how long it takes, each of us ensures that all pending tasks are closed that day. Special checkpoints for e-banking platforms are also regularly updated in our 'Bible' – the operating instructions compiled by our colleagues over the years. Each week, we will study any updates to this guidebook and work together to ensure high-quality payments.

I received the Five-Star Payment Craftsman award, but I have never felt like I deserved this title. It was my job to check every bit of payment and collection data, and verify process compliance. I have never done anything special. All of my colleagues in my team do exactly the same thing. Every one of us is committed to doing the best we can, from small details like filling in transaction notes and remarks on invoices, to major projects like bringing new systems online and finding ways to improve our processes. All of us are constantly thinking, discussing and sharing new ways of improving our work, to ensure the best possible payment process.

Every single employee is like a vector: we all have a magnitude and direction, but we are much stronger when we work as a team. It is the spirit of craftsmanship shared by the entire team that really makes our payments secure and our processes fast.

Dedication makes the ordinary sublime

After so many years serving as a bank account signatory, some colleagues who do the same job as me have asked, "Haven't you gotten bored yet, after doing the same thing over and over for so many years?"

This job isn't static, though. The company has accounts in many regional and national banks around the world. That means bank account signatories must stay up-to-date with new accounting rules and review the requirements of each country and region. The company's systems are also constantly changing. These changes may be subtle, but any negligence – even just related to the addition of a new field, the placement of a decimal point, or the difference between the left and right buttons on the approval page – could jeopardize the security of our funds.

Today, I still check each and every item on the payment approval checklist for each payment I make, never skipping a single one. Before I leave my seat or clock out, I examine my desk to make sure that all bank cards have been locked away. On the shuttle home, I review what I did that day in my head, trying to think of anything I forgot. If I think there may be something, I call a colleague who is still at work to double check. Before I go to bed, I check whether I have missed any messages or phone calls, because urgent requests may have come in. This may be a bit OCD, but I feel it's my responsibility to the job.

Over 20 years at Huawei, I have handled over one million payments safely and swiftly. These payments have underpinned the successful rollout of many mobile towers and optical fibres. I feel this is my tiny contribution to the Huawei vision of 'building a fully connected, intelligent world,' and it gives me a sense of pride in my work.

Huawei has given me a lot in terms of both monetary and non-monetary incentives. I feel lucky to have worked for the company. By the time you reach middle age, you know what you can do well and what you love. The function that I perform is quite ordinary, but I know that I can do it well. I think we must remain as committed to our jobs as we were on the first day. Then, in years to come, we can hold our heads up and say that we have done our part for this company, and for society as a whole.

The spirit of craftsmanship means that our time here has meant something.

Why Woks Are a Company Asset

By Shi Jian

In 2005, I was working as a cook at China's Investment and Trade Promotion Centre in the West African country of Côte d'Ivoire. One day, my boss came to me and said, "You'll need to make enough for a few extra people. A group of people from Huawei will eat with us for a while." It was the first time I had ever heard the name Huawei. I couldn't possibly have guessed that this company would become such a central part of my life, for the next decade and more.

Second helpings for everyone

A few months later, I was taken aside by Chen Lei, who was head of Huawei's Côte d'Ivoire Office at the time. "Shi Jian," he said, "we're building a staff canteen. What do you think about coming to work as the Huawei cook?" I had always liked the energy of this young Huawei team. The people at Huawei were not like anyone I'd worked with before. Plus, my contract at the Investment and Trade Promotion Centre was nearly up, so I didn't take much time to make the decision. Before long, I was packing up my belongings and moving to Huawei's Côte d'Ivoire Office.

There were already a dozen or so people working there, and they would all eat together. The task of equipping the canteen fell to me. I brought a secretary with me down to the market, and we threaded back and forth, buying all the kitchen utensils we needed. This was the first time I had been in charge of my own kitchen, and I was coming to realize just how much it took to run one. As the Chinese proverb goes, 'Even the smartest housewife can't make dinner without rice.'

The markets in Côte d'Ivoire didn't sell spatulas, woks, cleavers, or many other basic utensils of a Chinese kitchen. And, my French was terrible, so I had to describe everything I wanted to the secretary, who would then translate for the market vendors. In our quest for a simple Chinese kitchen cleaver, we were shown axes, hatchets, even shovels. In the end, we just had to make do with a large knife. The next few times I returned to China, I always brought a good stock of kitchenware back with me, though it made for some interesting times at airport security. In 2006, an employee called Zhang Haibing lugged a wok bigger than himself back from China for us, and that helped get us through the initial few months.

After arriving at Huawei I spent a couple of days getting set up, and then it was time to get down to business. We didn't even have tables and chairs yet, so everyone just grabbed their bowls and crouched together for the first couple of days. I still remember how on that very first day they were like starving men. Every single one of them came back for a second helping. Kitchen hygiene was hard to achieve in Africa, and there were no sterilizer cabinets to be bought in the entire country, so I did it the old fashioned way. I'd throw all the bowls and chopsticks into a big wok and sterilize them by boiling them in water. It was effective: no one ever got sick because of poor hygiene in my kitchen. This sterilization method kept us safe for years, until I was finally able to buy a proper sterilizer cabinet.

As Huawei expanded in Côte d'Ivoire, we needed more meat and seafood to keep all the new arrivals fed. The local supermarkets were expensive, and the produce was not always fresh, so every Saturday I started going with one of the Huawei employees down to the wet markets on the coast to buy our supplies.

Whoever came with me would tell me stories of long hours and of winning new contracts. It made me feel very proud. I thought, at the very least, if I can cook good meals, then I'm doing my part to help Huawei win those contracts.

Malarial expertise

In 2006, I had my first run-in with malaria. I thought I'd just caught a cold, so I took a few pills, strapped on a face mask and went into the kitchen as normal. But, as I stood there, stirring, my legs started to give way. A few times I almost fell headfirst into the wok, so I was forced to go back to my room to lie down. My head had hardly hit the pillow when I began burning up with fever. The general manager, Huang Yu, saw what had happened and quickly arranged for a car to drive me to the hospital. I ended up staying there for five days before I felt able to get out of bed. When the fever finally broke, my first thought was, "Everyone must be starving! It's been days. What have they all been eating?"

I picked myself up and sped back to the kitchen to fix everyone a proper meal.

But malaria was like a rite of passage. You weren't a real African hand until you'd had it once. Whenever someone new arrived from China, I would tell them about malaria prevention. And, whenever someone fell ill, I would keep an eye on their fever, and how they were feeling. I became quite expert at quickly diagnosing if they had malaria.

In 2007, we moved the canteen to a new building, and I exhausted myself with all the moving and setup work. I was run down, and malaria got me again. This time I knew what was coming, and I managed to recover a bit quicker. I contracted it a few more times over the following years. But, perhaps I'd built up some resistance, as I never had to go to hospital again. I would just take my pills, and take an injection in the evening, and I was able to keep working. Each time I shook off the disease in just a couple of days.

Since 2013, Huawei has made improvements in our office environment and our malaria prevention system in West Africa, and I have not had another bout of the illness. In fact, it's now rare for anyone in our office to get it.

500 dumplings in two hours

In the end, the Côte d'Ivoire Office grew so big that one cook could no longer keep up with the workload. The company sent us another cook, surnamed Deng, and then at the end of 2008, a third came, surnamed Yuan. Finally, we had a proper team, so we were able to teach each other a few new tricks and offer some new options. The team got a more exciting menu, and my own skills got a major boost.

Around this time, things took a distinct upturn for the Côte d'Ivoire canteen. Up until 2008, the company gave a fixed meal subsidy of US$5 per day to every employee in West Africa. To get a decent standard of food, everyone had to pay a little bit extra out of their own pockets. The five-dollar subsidy could be claimed back by employees who didn't eat in the canteen, either because they chose to cook for themselves or they were away visiting customers. But, a few people on the team would frequently skip meals just to save money. This wasn't a very healthy way to live at all. In February 2008, a new set of rules came into force. The meal subsidy was increased to US$15 per day, and the company stopped allowing staff to claim it in cash, to encourage everyone to eat together at the canteen. The new rules caused a celebratory mood to break out at the office – and the cooks joined in the jubilation! Prior to the change, we had only been able to make four dishes for each meal, but now we could do eight. Before, the best we could offer was shrimp, and now we could occasionally get a lobster!

Huawei cook Shi Jian

For Chinese employees stationed overseas, the Chinese New Year dinner was the biggest event of the year. The kitchen team would start preparations at least three days in advance. There was a substantial Chinese population in Côte d'Ivoire, and as the Chinese New Year approached, you had to make sure to get your order in early for a grouper or a lobster. Peanuts, sunflower seeds and rice crackers had to be bought at least half a month in advance.

Dumplings were the most time-consuming task of all. We would set aside time three days in advance and make at least two different kinds of filling. The other cooks would make the wrappers, and I'd set to making the dumplings. One year, though, we were never going to get them finished on time. Fortunately, some of the Huawei families living out there heard what was happening and came to the rescue. Soon enough we had a mass of people pitching in to help, and in two hours we were able to stuff 500 dumplings. With all this willing help, we were finally able to gather around the tables and eat our New Year meal together. We may have been in a distant patch of land, on the far shore of the Atlantic. We may also have been missing our families. But, we were warmed by the piping-hot dumplings we'd made ourselves at the turn of the Chinese New Year.

From that year on, families pitching in to help at Chinese New Year became standard practice. As a result, our dumplings always came in an interesting range of contrasting physiques. You might find 10 different shapes in the same bowl, making our dumplings as fun to look at as they were tasty to eat!

A full belly fuels a stout heart

At the turn of 2010–2011, there was political unrest in Côte d'Ivoire. Some staff and their families were evacuated back to China, leaving a small crew behind to hold down the fort. I volunteered to stay, to make sure that everyone still there got to eat properly. In March 2011, the situation unexpectedly deteriorated. There was gunfire in our neighbourhood; bullets flew over our compound. I snuck out and stocked up on enough rice, flour, vegetable oil and gas to make sure that all 26 employees who stayed could survive for a month. Every day, I would prepare a meal for everyone as quietly and inconspicuously as I could. More than anything, I was afraid of attracting attention to us.

During the worst two weeks of the crisis, we all kept ourselves locked securely away. Those with beds by the windows changed to other rooms. I remember that three stray bullets did fly into our compound. The worst smashed through a window and the curtains, and then ricocheted off the wall and landed right next to two of our guys, who were sheltering in a corner. Everyone was terrified, but every single person on that crew stuck it out. No one left; no one said they wanted to return to China. Those two guys just moved to a different desk and carried on with their work.

Woks are a company asset

Our office took a roll call twice a day, and gathered everyone for a safety meeting daily. As the man in charge of supplies, I had to go out every now and then to buy fresh food, and I must admit to feeling a little scared. But I thought to myself: I have to keep our three meals a day coming, to keep everyone's spirits up. If I get too scared to produce a square meal, they'll notice, and they'll think, "Even the cook's scared. We're done for!"

Just as the regime change was starting, a local driver was bringing one of our guys back to the compound. Before he could leave, word came that the government had fallen, and he had no choice but to stay with us. After two weeks, things had calmed down a little, and this driver and I made an expedition to the Chinese supermarket two kilometres away for condiments and crackers. We hired two armed guards to go with us. Outside the supermarket was the most horrible scene I had ever seen: the burning bodies of three soldiers in the middle of the road. One of the bodies was sitting up.

Soon after that, the airport was re-opened, and the company evacuated another 16 people. Ten of us remained behind. We were running low on rice, vegetables and everything else, and there was nothing to be bought in the city. We all rationed ourselves, but I made sure that I put three dishes and soup on the table at every meal. Every week I'd do a hotpot and make dumplings. When things seemed calmer, I'd slip out and search for supplies. In the end, our precautions paid off. We didn't suffer any casualties, and after another month, the worst was past and the city returned to normal.

Officially becoming a Huawei employee

2012 was a very good year for the kitchen crew. In West Africa, all of the canteen staff changed from being outsourced contractors to official employees of Huawei's subsidiary Smartcom. We had our own Huawei ID numbers, and were finally a real part of the team. I was so excited that I couldn't sleep for days.

In early 2013, we started a rotation system, and I was sent to Guinea for six months or so, and then to Abuja in Nigeria. I was surprised to find that many of the people I knew from Côte d'Ivoire had also ended up in Abuja. They grinned when they saw me: "At least we know what we'll be getting to eat, and we know that it will taste half decent!"

Chef Shi (middle) with some of his African friends

I have already been in West Africa for a decade. I came as a young man, and in Chinese they called me "Young Shi". Now I'm older than many of the Huawei staff here, and they call me "Old Shi". I gave my youth to this part of the world. In return, I've gained the friendship and respect of my Huawei colleagues. I've seen much in my time here, and learned a lot. It has been a good way to spend the last decade, I believe, and it has given me experience that I could not have gotten anywhere else.

I have never negotiated a sales contract, built a mobile tower, or signed a contract. But I have made sure that the Huawei team always has a good, hot meal on the table, and a hearty broth. I have made sure that their homesickness was eased by a full stomach. My life is bound to Huawei's success, too.

I've already turned 30 and, one day, I might leave Huawei, and bring my precious experience and unforgettable memories back home to China. I'd like to start my own restaurant, and I'll decorate it with pictures from my time in Africa. I have worked for Huawei in hardship regions, and I am proud of my experience!

Editors

Biography of
Tian Tao

Tian Tao is a member of the Huawei International Advisory Council, Co-Director of the Ruihua Institute for Innovation Management at Zhejiang University in Hangzhou, China, and Co-Director of the Cambridge Centre for Chinese Management at Cambridge Judge Business School.

In 1991, Mr. Tian founded *Top Capital*, the first Chinese magazine on private equity investment, and has served as Editor in Chief since.